The Christian Man:
Discussion and Application Guide

By

Patrick Morley

and

Joseph McRae Mellichamp

Thousand Fields Publishing
www.1000fieldspub.com

To Our Wives and Best Friends:

Patsy Morley

and

Peggy Mellichamp

The Christian Man:
Discussion and Application Guide

Introduction

To make sure *The Christian Man* scratches you where you itch, Pat gathered twenty-four men from twenty-four to forty-seven years of age (mostly mid-thirties) on a Saturday morning to storyboard the question, "What are the issues and topics that would make you feel *compelled* to pick up and read a book for men?" These men came from all walks of life and represent the racial and ethnic diversity of America.

When the dust settled, we had a list of ten issues that mattered most. That list formed the table of contents for *The Christian Man*. Then Pat asked them, "What are the questions you would most like to have answered or addressed about each of those topics?"

Storyboarding is a democratic process of brainstorming that ensures that each participant has an equal voice with all the others. *The Christian Man* is what emerged from that process.

Are you a student? A major challenge for students in a small group or class is taking notes of the important things the teacher covers. So for you, the *Discussion and Application Guide* for *The Christian Man* serves as an outline which can be annotated as the teacher covers the topics. Some years ago Rae came across the notes from the best professor he had in graduate school. He was so good, and entertaining, when Rae opened his old notes, there was virtually nothing in the notebook! He was too busy listening to take notes. We don't want that to happen. We want you to come away with the salient points ready at hand!

To make your experience as rewarding as possible, we have included in this *Discussion and Application Guide* a number of questions for each chapter in *The Christian Man*, to help you apply the chapter material. These are not simply fill-in-the-blank questions, but questions which will require you to think deeply about your life now and what you want your life to become. And also what you can to do to make the transformation happen.

Are you the teacher? The major challenge for teachers of any subject is to determine what the important points in a body of material are so that they can be covered thoroughly and well. So the *Discussion and Application Guide* can serve as your framework or outline. As you read through each chapter of the book, have a copy of the *Discussion and Application Guide* open and jot down examples, illustrations, and other teaching ideas in the margins as you go. Then, when you are done reading a chapter, you'll be set to present the ideas to your group.

Enjoy the journey!

Patrick Morley
Joseph McRae Mellichamp

Chapter 1. Identity: Settling Who I Am and What My Life is About

"Therefore, if anyone is in Christ, the new creation has come: The old has gone, the new is here!" 2 Corinthians 5:17

If they cut me, I want to bleed Jesus.

The Man in Room 3330

Ken was an eighty-year old patient in room 3330 of the local hospital. His buoyant, cheerful attitude was infectious and word about him had spread throughout the hospital. One morning a doctor appeared at his room and began reading his chart.
- The doctor asked Ken how he could be so upbeat and cheerful at his age in his condition.
- Ken responded with a question, "How do you find your enjoyment?"

The doctor replied that he didn't find much enjoyment in life. He had tried a plane and a boat, but neither helped. He continued that nothing he had ever done had given lasting satisfaction.

Ken replied that he knew what the doctor was saying and that the only thing that had ever given him lasting peace and satisfaction was a relationship with Jesus Christ.

Ken's prescription was corroborated by a Hispanic cleaning lady named Maria with whom Ken had spoken on several previous occasions.

The doctor could see that Maria had the missing thing for which he had been searching. And he wanted what Ken and Maria had found.

Over the next fifteen minutes Ken and Maria challenged the doctor to experience what they had found by asking Jesus to forgive his sins and to surrender his life to Jesus in faith.

Ken's Secret

Ken's secret was that he had settled it—who he was "in Christ" was who he really was.

- He was a disciple of Christ disguised as a paint salesman.
- He was able to live a passionate life for the glory of God.

What motivated the doctor to seek out Ken? What did he want? What do we all want?

What Men Want

We are all created to want three things:

- A cause—something we can give our lives to that will make a difference; our need to be significant, to find a purpose and a mission.
- A companion—someone to share life with. This is the area of relationships: love, family, friends, a wife.
- A conviction—a belief system or worldview that is true and coherent and makes sense of God and life.

Of the four worldviews—secular, moral, religious and Christian—all eventually fail except Christianity.

We could make a longer list of wants, but experience has shown that if one satisfies these three, everything else one wants or needs will be satisfied.

So here is the big idea or main point of this chapter: When you seek your identity in Jesus Christ and His gospel, you will find a deep lasting satisfaction so infectious that everyone else will want it too.

The questions "Who am I?" and "Why do I exist?" are not easy to answer and two important factors account for this.

Our Cultural Moment

First, men today are under a cloud of suspicion. Entertainment, news, and the social media have created a great mass of common assumptions about who men are—mostly negative.

But despite the assumptions, the truth is that most men try to do the right thing as they live out their lives, even though some men assuredly do pretty bad things.

And the good news is you can become the man God created you to be. God's promise is that you don't have to be constrained by the "contemporary outlook."

The Fall

Second, we must manage our lives against the Fall. Described in Genesis 3, the Fall refers to the account of how pervasive sin and suffering entered the world through the sins of Adam and Eve.

The Fall is an offense to human reason, but once accepted, it makes perfect sense of the human condition.
- It explains why we must do our work while feeling the prick of thorns.
- It helps us understand why we sometimes must suffer even as we enjoy the creation.

The Bible enables us to understand the forces which would prevent us becoming all that God intended for us to become. Three such forces are:
- The world which includes all approaches to life, work and family that conflict with Christianity. 1 John 2:15-17
- The flesh refers to our own sinful natures and results in immorality, theft, murder, adultery, greed and other such behaviors. Mark 7:20-23

- The devil who is intent on deceiving us, accusing us, and making us feel false condemnation, shame and guilt. He wants to rob us of our identity. John 8:44

Your Obituary Identity

When you see yourself, what do you see? What mental images come to mind?
- One of your roles—husband?
- Your work or ministry?
- What you have—home, money?
- What you look like—your appearance?
- Who you know—relationships?
- Who you are—your character and conduct?

Your "obituary" identity is the visible things people remember about you when you are gone.

The problem with this is what happens when these things no longer apply? Do you lose your identity?

Your "Naked Before God" Identity

Your true identity is the things that really matter when you take stock of your life—your wife, children, friends, faith, heart, your calling, character and conduct.

We call this your "Naked Before God" identity.

We are warned in Scripture about shallow thinking when it comes to identity. "The Lord said to Samuel, 'Do not consider his appearance or height, for I have rejected him. The Lord does not look at the things people look at. People look at the outward appearance, but the Lord looks at the heart.'" 1 Samuel 16:7

Scripture gives us the Christian answer to who we are and what our lives are all about. Psalm 8:3-4 sets the stage: "When I consider the heavens, the work of Your fingers, the moon, the

4

stars, which You have set in place, what is mankind that You are mindful of them, human beings that you care for them?" The answer:

- Our Identity—Who we are. "You have made them a little lower than God and crowned them with glory and honor." Psalm 8:5
- Our Purpose—What our lives are about. "You made them rulers over the works of Your hands: You put everything under their feet." Psalm 8:6

We were made to mirror God's identity—what theologians call the *imago dei*—the image of God. "Then God said, 'Let us make mankind in our image, in our likeness, so they may rule over the fish in the sea and the birds in the sky, over the livestock and all the wild animals, and over all the creatures that move along the ground.' So God created mankind in His own image, in the image of God He created them; male and female He created them." Genesis 1:26-27

Thus we see that our identity is to be a mirror of God's image and our purpose is to tend the culture and build His Kingdom!

Identity as "Roles"

We tend to think of ourselves along the lines of the different Roles we assume in our lives.

- Sons and Daughters.
- Friends.
- Temples.
- Charges.
- Disciples
- Servants.
- Vessels.

Identity as "Attributes"

Another way of thinking about identity is in terms of the kind of man I want to be in *character* and *conduct*—"attributes". And God has given us a complete list in Scripture in Galatians 5:22-23.

"But the fruit of the Spirit is love, joy, peace, patience, kindness, goodness, faithfulness, gentleness, self-control." And here is another—humility.

An important point in this regard: God's Spirit produces these attributes in our lives as we live our lives under His control.

A Hug and a Declaration

- Can I Give You a Hug?—God. God loves you very much. He wants to give you a hug. Over and over in Scripture we read of His love for us.
- A Call to Action: Something You Can Do for God. Here is an opportunity to declare your identity in Christ. Consider the Declaration and indicate your assent by signing it.

Application Questions

1. In Mainland China we learned that the present workforce in that large and booming country is intently focused on what they call the "Five Cs": Career, Cash, Companion, Car and Condo. Interestingly, only one of the "Five Cs" corresponds to the three presented in this chapter which are: Cause, Companion and Conviction. Do you understand why the Three Cs has the possibility of providing fulfillment and satisfaction while the Five Cs could never do so?

_____

_____

_____

_____

_____

2. The big idea for this chapter is "when you seek your identity in Jesus Christ and His gospel you will find a deep, lasting satisfaction so infectious that others will want it too." Another common way of expressing this is, "The chief end of man is to

glorify God and enjoy Him forever [Westminster Shorter Catechism]." What does this mean to you in terms of your ultimate identity and purpose?

_____

_____

_____

_____

_____

3. Reread the quote warning us of succumbing to the enticements of the world on page 28 of the text from 1 John 2:15-17. Reread the Five Cs in Question 1 above. Do you see the problem? Do you see why Cause and Conviction are so important to our identity and purpose? Begin now to flesh out what your Cause and Conviction need to be.

_____

_____

_____

_____

_____

4. Taken together, our Roles help to define our identity. Reflect on what your truly important Roles are or should be. Write them down and assess how you are doing with each.

_____

_____

_____

_____

_____

5. Attributes describe the kind of man we want to be in terms of character and conduct. A wonderful passage which is helpful in this regard is Deuteronomy 10:12-13, especially the command to "live in a way that pleases God." When we are walking with Christ and filled with His Spirit, the fruit of the Spirit is evident in our lives and this pleases God. Consider who you are, what you do,

and what you say. Is God pleased? Need to change anything? Use "Would this please God?" as a measure as you walk day by day.

_____

_____

_____

_____

_____

6. When we truly understand that God loves us it will change our lives. "You call me by name and tell me I have found favor with you. Please, if this is really so, show me Your intentions, so I will understand You more fully and do exactly what You want me to do. Exodus 33:12,13 NLB" When Moses became aware of his favor in God's eyes, he asked for two things: to understand God more fully (To know God) and do what God wanted of him (God's will). What are you doing to know God and to know God's will for your life?

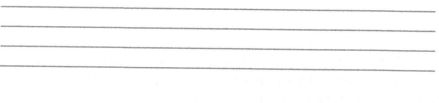

Chapter 2. Life Balance: How to Be Faithful with Everything Entrusted to Me

"Now it is required that those who have been given a trust must prove faithful." 1 Corinthians 4:2

You have all the time you need to do everything God wants you to do

Too Busy to Respond

Pat recalls the situation of James who didn't respond to any of Pat's voice mails over a period of weeks.

When they finally connected and Pat asked why James hadn't responded he replied with a half dozen reasons why he was too busy and concluded with the admission, "To be honest, I've just been so overwhelmed that I've felt paralyzed."

We all understand James' answer. In fact Life Balance was the second most important issue for the men who participated with Pat in posing the questions to be addressed in *The Christian Man*.

Here are some of the questions which surface:

- What should a typical day look like for a Christian man?
- How do I balance everyday life without losing focus on God and what's important?
- How do I prioritize effectively?
- In what ways can I get out of my normal routine and create a godly one?
- What are some tips to help me use my time better, especially for personal growth?
- I want everything I do to reflect Jesus. How do I:
  - Live a life that is integrated?
  - Separate my work and my family life?
- Are hobbies okay?

These are the questions of men who understand they have been given a trust—something to steward and guard. They want to be found faithful.

Most of us have more demands on our time than we have time to give—money, work, marriage, parenting, social and health pressures. And the pressures increase.

How can we juggle all the demands on our time, intellect, emotions, money, and relationships? What is a healthy mix?

Jesus and the Pressures of Life

When Jesus became a man, He emptied Himself taking the form of a bond-servant. He set aside His attributes as God and as a result He experienced many of the same pressures we do.

How did Jesus solve the "too much to do" problem? He was intentional. He took control of His calendar.

The big idea in this chapter is that like Jesus, you have all the time you need to do everything God wants you to do. We are going to help you settle what God wants to accomplish through you and for you. You will:
- Understand what priorities are and how they get set.
- Decide on and rank your own priorities.
- Complete a plan to help you:
  - Be intentional.
  - Control your calendar.
  - Live a balanced life.

What Are Priorities?

A priority is anything to which you assign a high degree of urgency or importance.
- Priorities are what we decide in advance matters most.
- Priorities precede goal setting and decision-making.

10

- Priorities can be daily, short term or long term.

The key, as with Jesus, is to determine our priorities in advance.

How Many Priorities Can One Man Juggle?

Would you agree that most men have too many priorities and the ones they have often conflict.

We know that men who can focus on doing a few things well tend to do better than those who can't.

And we also know that priorities necessarily change with the seasons of life.

What Are the Priorities of a Christian Man?

Here is a list of five biblical priorities that will help you manage pressures that will otherwise manage you.

1. Loving God. This is the unequivocal top priority for the Christian man.
   - Loving God is the first and greatest commandment.
   - Loving God is what matters most.
   - The more we love God, the more we want what He wants.
   Here are five ways we can enhance our love for God:
   - Knowing God. The turning point of our lives is when we stop seeking the God we want and start seeking the God who is. We can make Jesus Lord by bringing our entire lives under His authority,
   - Self Examination. John Calvin wrote, "Nearly all the wisdom we possess ... consists of two parts: the knowledge of God and of ourselves." We need to periodically examine ourselves to assess how we are doing.
   - The Bible. The single best way to know God is to read His bestselling book—the Bible. It is the Bible that enables us

11

to understand our personal experiences. God reveals Himself to us through His word.

- Prayer. Prayer is the currency of our personal relationship with Jesus. We are admonished in Scripture to "pray without ceasing."
- Church. Scripture also exhorts us to be involved in a local church: "and let us consider how to stimulate one another to love and good deeds, not forsaking our own assembling together..." Hebrews 10:24,25

2. Loving People. The second great commandment is, "Love your neighbor as yourself." The Christian man will love others.
    - Loving My Wife. Easily the number one problem most men face today is that their marriages are not working the way God intended. If my wife is truly the most important person in my life, I will spend time with her.
    - Loving My Children. No amount of success at the office can compensate for failure at home. So be your children's spiritual leader, greatest fan, encourager, cheerleader, champion, mentor and example.
    - Authentic Friendships. You will be fortunate in life if you have three real friends—men who genuinely care for you and accept you. Men who want the best for you and are willing to challenge you to get there with them.

3. Vocation. Vocation in the spiritual sense is a divine summons to serve God—it is what God is calling you to be and do.
    - The Job, Work. Most people will spend more time at work than any other place. You can be sure that if God has called you to spend forty, fifty, or more hours in a place, He wants you to have an impact there for Him.
    - Health, Leisure, Rest, Recreation. Health is a gift from God, but we are responsible to create a proper balance with rest, recreation, nutrition and exercise.

4. Money. Money, and how to handle it, needs to be a priority, which is probably why Jesus talked so much about it—fifteen

percent of the teaching of Jesus in the four gospels relates to money.

5. Ministry. Jesus prayed, "As You sent Me into the world, I have sent them into the world." John 17:18 God has given each of us one or more spiritual gifts with which to minister.

A Personal Self Assessment

A self assessment for each of the five major priorities is provided in the text to help you evaluate how you are doing in each area and, if desired to shuffle the priorities of each—after the first priority, of course.

The Starting Point to Adjust Your Priorities

The starting point here is not intuitively obvious. Here is why. I must first determine for each area what I really want. Understanding this enables me to ask the right questions to reshaping my priorities to what they ought to be.

For example, if loving God is not what I really want; it is not helpful to ask, "What do I need to do to love God more." The right strategy is to ask God to change my heart so that loving Him is the thing I really want above all else.

Squeezing Out Enough Time

Possibly the biggest obstacle to living a balanced life is squeezing out enough time. No man can do everything. Choices must be made.

Here is a great tip to help you invest your limited resources where they will count the most:

- Don't give yourself to those who don't absolutely need you at the expense of those who do.

13

- Or, put another way, prioritize everything you do on the basis of who's going to be crying at your funeral.

Getting the Right Things Done

Try listing the top priorities for the day—no more than ten things. Then start on number 1 and don't deviate until you finish it, then move on to number 2 and execute it completely without distraction. Then continue with number 3, number 4 and so on.

If items remain at the end of the day, move them to the top of your list for the next day. Following this approach ensures that you will always be working on your highest priorities.

The Power of a Specific Action Plan

Psychologists have a concept they call behavioral activation which is beginning any endeavor by taking a few simple steps in the right direction. It appears that this strategy includes its own positive reinforcement and can snowball.

A Call to Action

The call to action for this chapter is to set aside two or three hours for a personal retreat and to really focus on what you want your priorities and goals to be.

In this regard, you have been challenged to formulate twelve goals relating to the five biblical priorities of a Christian Man and to take a self assessment of how you are doing. You can do this in the time you are devoting to your personal retreat.

Application Questions

1. In *The Seven Habits of Highly Effective People* Stephen Covey groups activities into one of four quadrants: I. Important-Urgent, II. Important-Not Urgent, III. Not Important-Urgent, and IV. Not

Important-Not Urgent. It is really instructive to think of the activities of the Lord Jesus in the gospels in the light of this classification scheme. He spent most of His time in Quadrant II; a small amount in Quadrant I and none in Quadrants III and IV. Give an example of each of the quadrants from your own life. What does this say to you about activities on which you focus your energy and time?

_____

_____

_____

_____

2. Are you struggling at all with carving out regular time to spend with the Lord? Consider this thought from Matthew Henry's Commentary, "Why was man created at all, if not for the pleasure God receives from fellowship with His creation? It was for the very purpose of knowing Him that we were born. It's for knowing Him that you still live. When we're with Him, we fulfill the most basic longings within us. And we fulfill the deepest longing of God—that of our company. There's a special place in the heart of God that only you can fill. God is more than willing to be with you today. More than willing to hear your voice. God is more willing to be prayed to, and more ready to hear prayer than we are to pray." What is your reaction? What is your response?

_____

_____

_____

_____

3. Jesus said to His friend, "Martha, Martha, you are worried and bothered about so many things; but only a few things are necessary, **really only one**, for Mary [who was seated at the Lord's feet listening to His word] has chosen the good part which shall not be taken away from her." Luke 10:38-42 NLB Have you

discovered what Jesus characterized as your **"only necessary thing"**? What is it? What do you want to do in response to this?

_____

_____

_____

_____

4. Did you know it takes only fifteen minutes a day to read the Bible from cover to cover (Genesis to Maps) in one year—an average of 85 verses a day? When we discovered this, we individually determined to read thru the Bible every year for as long as we are able. Pat has read it cover to cover 30 times and Rae 21 times. Do you think you could find fifteen minutes a day? Would you like to give it a try?

_____

_____

_____

_____

5. Some years ago, I (Mellichamp again) was impressed along with two of my friends and our wives to develop a prayer journal, which we ultimately did—"*Audiences with the King*." Nothing earth shattering or elaborate, just a simple way of recording requests and God's answers. Such a journal takes practically no additional time or effort but pays huge dividends in terms of effectiveness and organization/permanence. Do you think this would help you in your prayer life? How so?

_____

_____

_____

_____

_____

6. One very helpful concept in terms of loving others is what is called the Spiritual Receptivity Continuum [Jim Engel and Wilbert Norton, *What's Gone Wrong with the Harvest?* Zondervan, 1975]. Imagine that every single person you meet is at some point on a line segment with a cross in the middle. On the left of the cross are unbelievers—who range from openly hostile to indifferent to interested; on the right of the cross are believers who range from baby Christians to growing Christians to mature Christians. Your job in loving others can be more focused if you assess where every person you meet is on the Spiritual Receptivity Continuum and what you can do to move them to the right. Think of two or three people you care about. Where are they on the continuum? How can you incorporate this concept in loving them?

_____

_____

_____

_____

_____

7. Would you agree that the marriages of most men are not working the way God intended? One reason for this may be that they are not speaking the same language their wives are. Gary Chapman lists five "love languages" in his book: Words of Affirmation, Physical Touch, Receiving Gifts, Quality Time, and Acts of Service. Quality Time is important—that is why it is featured in the Sample Goal in the text. Think about this concept and try to ascertain what your wife's love language is and set a goal which will affirm her love language.

_____

_____

_____

_____

_____

8. If you are like most men, work can become all-consuming. One day I (Mellichamp) was walking across campus reflecting on the

obituary of a prominent colleague I had read in the local newspaper the previous day. It listed all of his degrees, all the committee assignments he had had, all the papers and books he had written, and a few details about his family. I remember thinking, "all that stuff was important last week, but matters very little now." This led me to ask myself, "When I die, what would I want said of me." Here is what I decided and have followed since. "I want to be remembered as a professor who used his influence for Jesus in the lives of his students, his colleagues, and on the institution itself. I need to do all the other things well. If I'm not a good teacher, students won't care what I have to say. If I'm not succeeding in research, my colleagues won't care either. And I won't have a platform for influencing the institution." Does this help you when thinking about your job? How about you—what do you want said of you?

_____

_____

_____

_____

_____

9. In his great classic *The Training of the Twelve* (1871), A.B. Bruce writes, "The Sabbath was not a day taken from man by God with a demanding spirit, but a day given by God in mercy to man—God's holiday to His subjects. ... The best way to observe the Sabbath is that which is most conducive to man's physical and spiritual well-being—in other words that which is best for his body and soul. ... In light of this principle, you will keep the holy day in a spirit of intelligent joy and thankfulness to God the Creator for His gracious consideration toward His creatures." One cannot read this without being moved. What does this say to you about keeping the Sabbath? Will you? How?

_____

_____

_____

_____

18

10. Many Christians today have been influenced in their personal finances by R. G. LeTourneau and Dave Ramsey. LeTourneau, an industrialist of the Twentieth Century, after several unsuccessful attempts at running his own business, decided to make God his CEO. As a consequence he became very successful financially and he started giving more and more of his earnings to the Lord's work. Ultimately he was giving 90 percent of his income to the Lord and keeping 10 percent for himself. He quipped: it was a new form of tithing. Dave Ramsey, a Christian financial management speaker is big on saving and offers sound advice on managing financial resources God's way. Have you attended one of Dave Ramsey's seminars? If not would you consider doing so?

---

11. Os Guinness writes in his significant book *The Call: Finding and Fulfilling the Central Purpose of Your Life*, "The truth is not that God is finding us a place for our gifts but that God has created us and our gifts for a place of His choosing — and we will only be ourselves when we are finally there. God normally calls us along the line of our giftedness, but the purpose of giftedness is stewardship and service, not selfishness." Does this motivate you to understand your spiritual giftedness and investigate how God has called you minister in response?

Chapter 3. Growth: Becoming a More Kingdom-Minded Man

"And the things you have heard from me in the presence of many witnesses entrust to reliable people who will also be qualified to teach others." 1 Timothy 2:2

A Bible, a small group, and serving someone else will solve 90 percent of your problems.

First-timers

Pat shares his experience in meeting frequently with first time attendees at his Friday morning The Man in the Mirror Bible Study. He asks each one to answer the question, "Where are you today on your spiritual journey?" And their answers can be grouped in three categories:

- Seekers or Inquirers are those who really don't know God yet in a personal way through Jesus but are drawn to investigate the Christian faith.
- New Christians are those who have recently made a profession of faith and who want to discover, "What did I just sign up for?"
- Then there are long-time Christians who have known God for some time, but are sensing a need to mobilize or remobilize. They believe they need a more biblical Christianity.

As different as they are, what all these men have in common is a deeply felt hunger to know more about God. And this hunger to grow spiritually was the number one issue cited by the men who provided input for *The Christian Man*.

The Goal of Spiritual Growth

What is the next right step for anyone desiring to know God more intimately? Jesus answered the question in some of His last words before returning to heaven:

"All authority in heaven and on earth has been given to Me. Therefore go and make disciples of all nations, baptizing them in the name of the Father and of the Son and of the Holy Spirit, and teaching them to obey everything I have commanded you. And surely I am with you always, even to the very end of the age." Matthew 28:18-20

So the goal of spiritual growth, revealed in what we call the Great Commission, is to become a disciple of Jesus—to follow Him. Understanding this, one should ask what is a disciple and how do we become one?

What is a Disciple, and How Do You Become One?

The Greek word for disciple (*mathetes*) means "pupil" or "learner." And it has come to mean one who follows and adheres to the person and teachings of Jesus.

Here is a good way to think about what it means to be a disciple of Jesus. A disciple is:

- *called* to live "in" Christ (knowing God, salvation, abiding)
- *equipped* to live "like" Christ (knowing *about* God, spiritual growth, renewing the mind)
- *sent* to live "for" Christ (Neighbor love and deeds, living powerfully by the biblical priorities you set in Chapter 2)

Let's elaborate on the three attributes.

Called to Live "In Christ"

In theology, "knowing God" pertains to the Greek word *kerygma*, which stands for the proclamation of the gospel. It's knowing enough about the birth, life, death, and resurrection of Jesus to believe the good news through faith and repentance. So the first step to become a disciple is to believe the *kerygma*, often called the "elementary teachings."

21

At some point, most followers want to go beyond the elementary teachings. He senses an urge to grow in maturity, love, knowledge, wisdom, humility and power. He wants to experience and exhibit all the fruit of the Holy Spirit—love, joy, peace, patience, kindness, goodness, faithfulness, gentleness, self-control. Galatians 5:22,23. He wants to know God and know *about* God.

Equipped to Live "Like Christ"

The Greek word *didache* (teachings) is the part of theology focused on knowing about God. Many of us would say, "I have put my faith in Christ—I *know* Him. Now I want—no need—to know more *about* Him."

We need the teachings. They tell us what we want to know about God and they give us wisdom and guidance for our marriages, families, friendships, work, sexuality, culture, and personal ministries—the seven topics which are the subjects of the remaining chapters of *The Christian Man*.

Sent to Live "for Christ"

As we grow in our relationship with Christ, our focus should shift from ourselves to others. We begin to desire to share what we know about Jesus with others.

Dwight Moody heard, "The world has yet to see what God will do with and for and through and in and by the man who is fully and wholly consecrated to Him." Moody determined to be that man.

Here is how it happens.

Spiritual Disciplines: The Portal to Spiritual Growth

In his Letter to the Ephesians, Paul explained the importance of spiritual maturity and how it is fostered in the church:

- "He gave some as apostles, and some as prophets, and some as evangelists, and some as pastors and teachers, for the equipping of the saints for the work of service..." Ephesians 4:11,12
- "Until we all attain to the unity of the faith, and of the knowledge of the Son of God, to a mature man, to the measure of the stature which belongs to the fullness of Christ." Ephesians 4:13
- "As a result, we are no longer to be children, tossed here and there by waves and carried about by every wind of doctrine, by the trickery of men, by craftiness in deceitful scheming." Ephesians 4:14

Much of the growth described in this book is accomplished through spiritual disciplines, which are the regular habits of men (and women) who are being called, equipped, and sent to live in, like, and for Jesus.

Any regular practice that draws you to abide in Christ and Him in you, love others as Christ loves you, or bear much fruit is profitable for becoming a mature and equipped disciple.

When it comes to spiritual growth, Pat distills what he has learned about helping men grow to the one idea: A Bible, a small group and serving someone else can help you become more kingdom-minded, solve your problems and help you become the hero of your own story.

Let's see how.

The Bible

Everyone has questions about the Bible. Here are just a few:
- How could you get all those animals in one boat?
- What kind of God would tell a man to kill his own son (Abraham and Isaac)?
- How can a man be swallowed by a fish and live for three days?

- How could a virgin have a baby?

For a mature believer, perhaps 5 percent of the Bible is mysterious. But 95 percent is perfectly understandable. Why would one let the few things that baffle him spoil or overshadow the 95 percent that presents a crystal-clear, concise, coherent, easily understood, and believable story?

The Bible tells us we have a loving Father who relentlessly pursues His wayward children until we reconcile with Him, and once we return, watches over us through thick and thin.

Why Is There Such Little Power Here?

For sure, the Bible is daunting. At roughly 780,000 words, that's about 2,500 pages—equivalent to about twelve non-fiction books.

With only 10 percent of people reading the Bible with any regularity, biblical illiteracy accounts for the lack of power for many Christians.

One day some of the religious leaders, attempting to trick Jesus, asked Him a question about the resurrection. His reply was, "Your problem is that you don't know the Scriptures, and you don't know the power of God." Matthew 22:29

Knowing Scripture releases the power of God.

Interpreting the Bible

To grow God's way, we need to be scrupulous to interpret the Bible based on what the original authors wrote, intended, and meant.

We should use the Bible to interpret our experience, not our experience to interpret the Bible. This is the difference between being a biblical Christian or a cultural Christian.

First Step: Start (or Reboot) a Quiet Time

Nothing else will make you feel as close to God as a time of consistent private devotions, and when inconsistent or absent, nothing will make you feel farther away.

If you don't already have a consistent devotional time alone with God, start by setting aside a few minutes each day to read a chapter of the Bible and to say a prayer.

A good approach for organizing your prayer time is to use the ACTS acrostic as follows:
- Adoration. Worship God for His attributes.
- Confession. Confess your sins and ask for forgiveness.
- Thanksgiving. Express gratitude for blessings and mercies.
- Supplication. Make your requests to God.

Take the Challenge: Read Through the Bible in One Year

It only takes about fifteen minutes a day to read through the entire Bible—an average of about 85 verses a day. Commit to read through the Bible this year.

This is such a rewarding endeavor that both Pat and Rae have resolved to continue to complete this each year for as long as they are able. Pat has completed 30 consecutive readings and Rae 21 consecutive readings.

Set a Routine

What is the best time of day, place, frequency, and amount of time for you to read the Bible? It is a good idea to have a set schedule, but realize there will be times when you have to shuffle things around.

How much time you spend is completely a matter of personal preference. It may vary from five minutes to an hour a day.

Pray When Reading

A life of devotion is communing with God; a life of study leads to knowing God. We want loving and knowing God to be our highest aspirations.

Oswald Chambers wrote, "Unless in the first waking moment of the day you learn to fling the door wide back and let God in, you will work on a wrong level all day..."

What to Do When Your Mind Wanders

When I am reading Scripture, if I am convicted of a sin or prompted to do some good deed, I assume that's the Spirit speaking to me and I listen and act.

If I am entertaining untoward thoughts, I assume that the world, the flesh or the devil is behind these and I reel them in as quickly as possible and refocus on positive things.

What You Can Do When You Get Stuck

Almost everyone gets bogged down at some time or another. It may be that a section of Scripture is just tough slogging through—Leviticus or Numbers. Or perhaps you have fallen behind in your reading schedule.

What should you do? Keep on keeping on, was how legendary coach Bear Bryant challenged his players. It is appropriate here—it will change. If you get way behind, it may be best to punt it and start over again.

The bottom line is that God would rather spend a little time with you in His word than no time at all.

A Small Group

Someone once asked Billy Graham what his plan of action would be if he were pastor of a large church in some city. He answered, "I would get a small group of eight to ten or twelve men with whom I could share everything I know. Then I would have that many laypeople who could teach what they had learned to eight or more others."

Jesus Himself used a small group as His venue for spiritual growth. He launched His divine plan to redeem mankind by making disciples of twelve men. This was His primary discipleship model. Why was that?

Why Small Groups?

Jesus knew that most meaningful change takes place in the context of small group relationships—men sharpening men with truth, encouraging each other for the daily battle, and sticking with each other over the long haul.

Studies suggest that less than ten percent of men are involved in any kind of ongoing discipleship.

What Can You Get in a Small Group That You Can't Get Any Other Way?

The thing that makes small groups special is that the size is manageable. You feel like you can really get to know the others. And you feel like they can get to know you well enough that they really understand you and care about what happens in your life. What kind of small group is right for you? You want a group that feels like you are coming home to a family that really cares about you.

What should a small group do? There are many possibilities, but the bottom line is that you are "doing life together." You'll

27

study the Bible together, pray for one another, hold each other accountable, and check on each other when appropriate. It's called "life-on-life-discipleship."

Serving Someone Else

Every Christian man is to have a personal ministry. "For we are God's handiwork, created in Christ Jesus to do good works which God prepared in advance for us to do." Ephesians 2:10

Serving someone else is one of the chief identifying marks of a disciple. "This is to My Father's glory, that you bear much fruit, showing yourself to be My disciples." John 15:8

We pursue service based on the way God has wired us with the gifts of the Holy Spirit. [You will be completing an assessment to enable you to ascertain what your particular gift(s) is/are. Following is a listing of the specific gifts.]

Service Gifts
- Mercy
- Hospitality
- Administration
- Faith
- Service
- Giving
- Leadership
- Discernment

Speaking Gifts
- Knowledge
- Preaching
- Evangelism
- Shepherding
- Wisdom
- Teaching
- Apostleship
- Encouragement

Signifying Gifts
- Tongues
- Miracles
- Interpretation of Tongues
- Healing

Becoming aware of your own spiritual gifts will (1) help you understand how and where you fit into the body of Christ, (2) help you set priorities for service, and (3) give you direction for developing a personal ministry.

Application Questions

1. Why do you suppose it is that spiritual growth is so high on the agenda of many Christians today? Do you suppose God plants a desire to be mature in each of His children? Consider what might be called the personal mission statement of the Apostle Paul in Colossians 1:28 NLB, "And we proclaim Him, admonishing every man and teaching every man with all wisdom that we may present every man complete (mature) in Christ." Maturity was at the very top of Paul's agenda too! What do you need to do in your life to clear the decks, so to speak, in order that you can truly make this your top priority?

_____

_____

_____

_____

_____

2. Paul wrote to the Corinthian believers, "I could not speak to you as to spiritual men, but as to men of flesh, as to babes in Christ. I gave you milk to drink, not solid food, for you were not able yet to receive it..." 1 Corinthians 3:1-2 NLB. Ouch! That hurts. Of course he is referring to their level of spiritual maturity. And we certainly don't want anyone to think of us in these terms, do we? Do you need a plan to become spiritually mature? What are some ideas to grow that appeal to you?

_____

_____

_____

_____

3. Dallas Willard writes in his book, *The Divine Conspiracy*, in answering the question, what would motivate a person to choose to become a disciple of Jesus, "Obviously, one would feel great admiration and love, would really believe that Jesus is the most magnificent person who has ever lived. One would be quite sure that to belong to Him, to be taken into what He is doing throughout this world so that what He is doing becomes your life, is the greatest opportunity one will ever have." Do you believe this? Does this motivate you to want to be more Kingdom-Minded?

_____

_____

_____

_____

_____

4. My own experience (Rae) in this regard was that I was not discipled until 13 years after I trusted Christ with my life, even though I was in church every Sunday for those thirteen years. Unfortunately, the churches my wife and I attended didn't "do discipleship." The goal of *The Christian Man* is to help you become spiritually mature. The text material and the questions in the text and in the *Discussion and Application Guide* were structured with that end in mind. The small group format is incorporated to facilitate that. Your small group leader wants that to happen. But ultimately, you are responsible for doing whatever is necessary to mature spiritually. Does this motivate you to develop a plan for growing spiritually? What will you do? Do you see the importance of accountability?

_____

_____

_____

_____

_____

5. At a Christian conference, the middle-aged leader of one of the sessions, a man who had been around the block a few times, made

the comment, "most Christians are 'on the Take.'" What he meant was they are mainly looking out for themselves. Many pastors confirm that "consumerism" is a huge problem in the church today. When we begin to be more concerned for the needs of others than we are for ourselves, we are beginning to grow spiritually. "Sent to Live for Christ," is all about serving others. What can you do now to become more of a giver instead of a taker?

_____

_____

_____

_____

_____

6. Obviously, the Bible is fundamental to our spiritual growth, but what about the things in the Bible that we don't understand? Everyone has questions about the Bible. Josh McDowell wrote a book titled, *Answers to Tough Questions Skeptics Ask about the Christian Faith*. In our experience, the questions people raise, whether they are biblical amateurs or hardened critics, tend to be the same ones again and again. With some preparation and practice, you will be able to come up with satisfying answers to most of the queries about the Bible you are likely to encounter. And, as we have written, why let the few things that baffle us spoil or overshadow the 95 percent that presents a crystal-clear, concise coherent, easily understood, and believable story? Start a list of tough questions and answers here.

_____

_____

_____

_____

_____

7. The problem is that we live such hectic lives, filled with so much activity, that some days it is just impossible to set aside time to spend in God's word. Rae: "One night twenty years or so ago I was watching Monday Night Football when it occurred to me that I

hadn't spent time in the Word that day. I protested to myself that I was just really busy and my busyness had prevented me. As I reflected on this, I realized that I usually watched Monday night football, a college game (or two) on Saturday, a pro game on Sunday, and I was really happy when they started doing Thursday night football! I was spending fifteen plus hours a week watching football on TV and protesting that I was too busy to spend an hour a day in fellowship with the God of the Universe in His Word! This is DUMB! I determined then and there that I would make spending time with the Lord in His word my number one priority every day for the rest of my life. I may have missed two or three days in the twenty or so years since." Can you think of anything short of a legitimate emergency that is more important than spending time with God in His word? I can't. What do you think? Are there some things you could cut out of your schedule in order to give fellowship with the Lord its rightful place in your life?

_____

_____

_____

_____

8. We advise that you set a routine for your devotional time by having a set time of day which is best for you. Here is one important caveat. Regardless of how well we plan our days, there will always be unforeseen occurrences which necessitate shuffling our schedules around. Not a problem. What is a problem is when you double-book and then skip your time with God—especially if it becomes a habit. Do you have routine devotions? How often do you skip? Do you plan to "do it later?" What usually happens when you say that? Do you want to be more consistent? What would it take for that to happen?

_____

_____

_____

_____

9. Serving someone else is one of the chief identifying marks of a disciple. Consider again the Os Guinness quote from the last chapter. "The truth is not that God is finding us a place for our gifts but that God has created us and our gifts for a place of His choosing—and we will only be ourselves when we are finally there. ... *God normally calls us along the line of our giftedness, but the purpose of giftedness is stewardship and service, not selfishness.*" Does this motivate you to ascertain what your spiritual gift(s) is/are and to use it/them in serving? What will you do as a result?

_____

_____

_____

_____

_____

10. A process for discovering your spiritual giftedness is outlined in *The Christian Man*. There are also some automated tools which will help you accomplish this goal. Perhaps you and the other guys in your small group could investigate some of these and check out one or more of them. What do you think? Here a link to one such tool: [perimeter.org/pages/worship/spiritual-gifts-analysis/]

_____

_____

_____

_____

_____

Chapter 4. Marriage: Finding a New Best Friend in Your Wife

"He who finds a wife finds what is good and receives favor from the Lord." Proverbs 18:22

Most marriage problems would disappear if we would simply speak to our wives with the same kindness, courtesy, forethought, and respect with which we speak to our coworkers.

What Needs to Happen Now That the Honeymoon Is Over

Once the honeymoon is over it's a new season to settle down, set up a home, build a life together, understand each other's needs, synchronize your lives and find a rhythm for living together. Here are just a few of the questions we must answer:
- What's going to be the division of labor in our home?
- How are we going to support each other?
- What is my mate's love language?
- How can we best encourage, comfort, and console each other and take the time to do that.

And here are a few of the other challenges newlyweds face:
- What will our sex life be like?
- What about children: How many and when?
- Figuring out how to deal with money.
- Learning how to resolve conflicts.
- Learning how to ask for and give forgiveness.
- Learning how to make time to have fun together.

Author Florence Littauer wrote about these adjustments saying, "We are attracted to each other's strengths, but then go home to live with each other's weaknesses.

The #1 Problem and the #1 Opportunity for Most Men

If we put men's marriage problems in one stack and all the other problems men face in a second stack, the marriage stack alone is higher than all of men's other problems combined. And easily the number one problem for most men is that their marriages are not working the way God intended.

But there is more. The issues most couples struggle with during their first year of marriage are, by degrees, the same issues they'll still be struggling with five, ten, or twenty years down the road.

The number one opportunity for most married men is how a surprisingly few, but strategic, course corrections can dramatically alter where your marriage will end up in ten or twenty years. Here's how.

Why Men Get Married

Many try to explain why men get married. God supplied the best answer at the creation when He said, "It is not good for the man to be alone. I will make a helper suitable for him." Genesis 2:18 And, "That is why a man leaves his father and mother and is united to his wife, and they become one flesh." Genesis 2:24

Men don't like to be alone. It's in our nature. And we need help. That's also in our nature. Marriage is the beautiful, mysterious fusion of a man and a woman into what the Bible intriguingly calls "one flesh."

By doing marriage God's way, you can be your wife's best friend, and she yours.

The Way God Made Her

Genesis 3:16 says, "To the woman He said, "I will make your pains in childbearing very severe; with painful labor you will give birth to children. Your desire will be for your husband, and he will rule over you." As part of her nature, your wife is going to give you the first place in her life. A wife's greatest need is for intimacy with her husband. That's her natural instinct.

35

Because of the Fall, her desire for you can be corrupted or exploited. She might be susceptible to manipulation, jealousy, being too clingy, too needy, worry, or wanting to control. Here are a couple of appropriate biblical admonitions to husbands:

- "Husbands, love your wives and do not be harsh with them." Colossians 3:19
- "Husbands, in the same way be considerate as you live with your wives ..." 1 Peter 3:7

In other words, cut her some slack. Just as you need her support when life is tough (because of the Fall), she needs you to be tender with her.

Sacrificial Love Is Your Primary Role

Pat shares the story of how his wife's parents moved to Orlando for the last years of their lives and how his mother-in-law had to move into the extended care wing of their retirement community shortly thereafter. Pat's father-in-law, Ed, made his wife his top priority spending as much time as possible with her and because of that, they were best friends.

The primary instruction the Bible gives about man's role as husband is, "Husbands, love your wives, just as Christ loved the church and gave Himself up for her to make her holy, cleansing her by the washing with water through the word, and to present her to Himself as a radiant church, without stain or wrinkle or any other blemish, but holy and blameless. In this same way, husbands ought to love their wives as their own bodies. He who loves his wife loves himself." Ephesians 5:25-28

Most marriage problems would disappear if we would simply speak to our wives with the same kindness, courtesy, forethought and respect with which we speak to our coworkers. Here are some practical ideas to help you do just that—adopting the 70 percent

36

mindset, praying for and with your wife, and making deposits into her emotional bank account

The 70 Percent Mindset

The first suggestion to help you make your wife your top priority is to adjust your expectations. If you set realistic expectations, you won't feel like you are getting less from each other than you expected. What is realistic?

Pat cites statistics which suggest that even the best marriages operate only at about 70 percent of potential. Even the best marriages will be trouble free only about 70 percent of the time. And the Fall (sin) is the reason for this. Accepting this, we should be okay with some rough patches and cut each other some slack.

And here is how we work that out on a practical level. We adopt the guiding principle in our marriage relationship, "I let you be you and you let me be me." In other words, let your wife be herself, even if that is not what you would do in a given situation. And she should do the same.

Pray for Your Wife

Here is a prayer which expresses, in general, what is being suggested here. It's called "The Marriage Prayer."

Father,
We said, "'Til death do us part"—We mean it.
We love You more than each other, and each other more than anyone or anything else.
Help us bring each other into Your presence today.
Make us one, like You are threeinone.
We want to hear each other, cherish each other, and serve each other—so we both would love You more and bring You glory.
Amen.

Be sure to reread the evolution of the prayer in the book from the original "me" centered to the final "pro" version given above. It is instructive.

Pray with Your Wife

In addition to praying for your wife, you can also pray with her. Surprisingly not many men actually pray with their wives. We don't want to be in that company!

Here are some suggestions:
- How long will this take? A few minutes a day.
- You don't need a special time or place—wherever, whenever.
- You can pray for anything you want or need.
- Always pray for family members—children, grandchildren.
- Always pray over meals—Jesus did.

This doesn't take a lot of effort, but it can make a profound difference.

Praying the Marriage Prayer with Your Wife

Pat prays the "Marriage Prayer" *for* his wife nearly every day; he prays the prayer *with* his wife once or twice a month.

Here is his assessment: "I can't think of anything that has warmed my heart toward my wife and made me feel more connected with her than praying this prayer with her out loud."

The Emotional Bank Account

Every human being—you, your wife, or the woman you are going to marry—has an emotional bank account. Every interaction you have with her you are either making a deposit into her emotional bank account or a withdrawal. Everything about your relationship is either a deposit or a withdrawal. Some examples:

- After a tough day at work, you growl, "Whatever you've had to go through, I've had to go through a lot worse, so don't bother me." A withdrawal!
- The next morning, feeling guilty for being so grumpy, you decide to bring her breakfast in bed with an apology. A deposit!

You need to need to focus your deposits where your wife most appreciates them. To accomplish this, you need to know her love language.

Gary Chapman identifies in his book *The Five Love Languages* the ways in which people express and experience love. They are:
- Words of Affirmation
- Quality Time
- Receiving Gifts
- Acts of Service
- Physical Touch

Our tendency is to love the way we want to be loved, not necessarily the way the way our mate wants to be loved. So study your mate to determine which is her primary love language.

By coupling the emotional bank account with the five love languages you have a focused way of making deposits.

Be Your Wife's Best Friend

When asked to identify the most important issues they face in their marriages wives often respond with "We don't spend enough time together," and "When we are together, our conversations need to be more meaningful." Time and talk—these are the issues on the minds of many wives.

Perhaps the biggest deposit you can make to your wife's bank account and the thing that will communicate that you want to love her sacrificially, that you want her to be your top priority after God, is to say, "I want to be my wife's best friend."

And a good way to begin is to just linger around the dinner table for twenty minutes to just talk. Listen without giving an overly quick reply. Just really getting to know or re-know this fragile flower who has been entrusted to you, a woman who wants intimacy, who is vulnerable with a desire for you. Just spend time with her.

A Call to Action

One day there will just be the two of you. The kids will be grown and gone. There will be only two rocking chairs sitting side by side.

Doesn't it make sense to invest today in the woman who is going to be sitting next to you then? Which of the ideas you have seen in this chapter will you make your call to action?

Application Questions

1. It is unfortunate that most people enter marriage with little or no preparation. Perhaps you had good parental role models in this regard. Or you may know some couples who appear to have solid marriages. Become a student of your parents or friends with good marriages. What makes a good marriage?

_____

_____

_____

_____

_____

2. Pat suggests that the number one problem for most men is that their marriages are not working the way God intended. Is this true of you? Jesus referred to God's original intention for marriage in

Matthew 19:8. What did God intend for marriage? See Genesis 2:18-25

_____

_____

_____

_____

_____

3. It is suggested that the issues most couples struggle with during their first year of marriage are the same ones they will be struggling with five, ten, or twenty years down the road. Finances is certainly one of the persistent issues of contention. Can you suggest others? Any that might be unique to particular periods?

_____

_____

_____

_____

_____

4. "As part of her 'nature' your wife is going to give you the first place in her life?" If you really think about this, it is absolutely deserving of our best response in return. What are some of the ways you can and will respond to your wife for giving you first place in her life?

_____

_____

_____

_____

_____

5. Can you think of some simple rules of thumb which if you observe will prevent you from speaking harshly to or being inconsiderate of your wife? What about never responding to an angry comment in kind? What about always being mindful of her position as weaker vessel—holding doors open for her, carrying in the groceries, etc., etc? You might want to memorize these!

_____
_____
_____
_____
_____

6. We are admonished to love our wives as Christ loved the church. Wow! This is a high standard! He gave Himself up for her to make her holy. How are you doing with this? What are some ways you can sacrificially give of yourself in order to make your wife holy? Could you encourage her somehow in her spiritual walk? Could you be more enthusiastic in supporting her activities with women friends? Think this through and follow through.

_____
_____
_____
_____
_____

7. The big idea for this chapter is to speak to our wives with kindness, courtesy, forethought, and respect. Think of how you treat the people at work. Need to change how you treat your wife? What does it mean to treat her with kindness? Courtesy? What about forethought? That implies that you have thought about your treatment of her before. Have you? Do you respect your wife? How do you communicate that?

_____
_____
_____
_____
_____

8. What we often try to do in our marriages is recreate our spouse in our own image. We try to make her do and say and think exactly like we do. Racecar driver Larry Dixon said, "If two people were exactly alike one of them would be unnecessary." Do you

understand why "I'll let you be you and you let me be me" is so important?

_____

_____

_____

_____

_____

9. Pat writes, "I realized most of my prayers were in the 'key of me.'" Is this true of you? Some years ago, I (Rae) became so convicted about the 'me centeredness' of my prayers, that I decided to rearrange my prayer life putting God's "things" ahead of my own requests. So now, I pray for the things I know are on God's heart and the hearts of others before making my own requests. I even arrange my written requests which I write down daily with God's stuff first and then my own. How do you pray?

_____

_____

_____

_____

_____

10. I (Rae) can't tell you how important it is for you to determine what your wife's love language is and to respond accordingly. For years I was knocking myself out making deposits to her emotional bank account by doing Acts of Service. Then one day after attending a Book Study on Gary Chapman's book *The Five Love Languages*, she informed me that her love language was Words of Affirmation. I promptly read the book and am trying to be more affirming. Anyone need some surplus Acts of Service? What is your wife's love language?

_____

_____

_____

_____

_____

11. For fifteen years my wife and I (Rae) worked full-time with the faculty ministry of Cru (Campus Crusade for Christ). We had helped start the ministry 25 years earlier. In the years of full-time ministry we made over 200 campus visits together, giving 500 plus talks at 130+ universities and colleges in 15 countries. We had determined to do this together. Peggy missed only one of the trips we made—because of her mother's health. Spending time together works. How can you do so?

_____

_____

_____

_____

_____

12. I (Rae) have heard lots of wives say, "I married him for better or worse but not for lunch!" Whenever I hear this sentiment expressed, I am saddened because I was fortunate to work only a mile from our home for 25 years and we had had lunch together for most days during those years. Especially when our children were young and in school, it was a great time to be alone together and to talk about really significant things. Most couples probably can't do lunch together, but when can you carve out some quality time on a regular basis to have meaningful conversation?

_____

_____

_____

_____

_____

Chapter 5. Children: A Dad Who Really Makes a Difference

"Folly is bound up in the heart of a child." Proverbs 22:15

"Yes I love you, and, no, you can't have your own way."

The Un-Discipled Dad

Pat begins this chapter on the importance of dads in the lives of their children by sharing some personal details of his own family growing up.
- His grandfather abandoned his family when his father was two.
- His father started working to support the family at age six.
- His father stuck it out with his family even though it was hard.
- His father had no models of what a father should be.
- His father was unprepared at Pat's rebellion as a teen-ager.

Proverbs 22:15 says, "Folly is bound up in the heart of a child, but the rod of discipline will drive it far away." Every child starts out foolish and Pat's father had no model for discipline. He apparently had no training, no instruction, no discipleship, and he didn't have a group from which to get advice in fathering.

As a result, Pat grew up with a chip on his shoulder, which ultimately led to his father encouraging him to enlist in the U.S. Army. And the Army dispensed the discipline that his father was not equipped to give him.

The purpose of this chapter is to give you the basic training on how to father your children in a way that will really make a difference for them.

What Our Kids Really Need

The challenging mission of a Christian father is to provide enough structure to drive out the folly, while never letting your children have any reason to doubt that you unconditionally love and accept them.

The quote, "Yes I love you, and, no, you can't have your own way," can help us find the right balance. Almost every parenting error is the result of getting one or both of the admonitions out of kilter.

- The *Authoritarian* Father: "No, I don't love you, and no, you can't have your own way."
- The *Permissive* Father: "Yes, I love you, and yes, you can have your own way."
- The *Disconnected* Father: "No, I don't love you, and yes, you can have your own way."
- The *Encouraging* Father: "Yes, I love you, and no, you can't have your own way."

The Encouraging Father is the pattern which will guide you to the right balance between structure and discipline.

Your Parenting Style

Every father wants to know, What does it mean to be too strict? If I am too strict what will happen? What does it mean to not be strict enough? If I am too permissive, what will happen?

When it comes to providing structure there are two possible errors. The first is too much structure which can lead to legalism. The second is not enough structure which can lead to fear or uncertainty.

What is the right balance? There are two fathering styles: fathering for performance and fathering the heart.

- Many dads father for performance. They focus on external behavior and try to get their children to "do the right things." Scripture warns, "Fathers, do not exasperate your children, instead bring them up in the training and instruction of the Lord." Ephesians 6:4

- Fathering the heart is the approach the Bible recommends. It is to look not only at the behavior but also at the reasons beneath the behavior. "For the mouth speaks what the heart is full of." Matthew 12:34

You can raise your children under grace or law, but grace is better. If you raise them with too much structure they are likely to reject what you have tried to teach them when they are on their own.

Here is a simple rule to help you balance structure: *Do not allow what God prohibits and do not prohibit what God allows.*

Practical Ideas

Here are some very practical ways you can embed this principle in your family's dynamic.

Love Their Mother

Theodore Hesburgh, former president of the University of Notre Dame said, "The most important thing a father can do for his children is to love their mother."

And sociologists tell us that the best predictor of healthy children is a healthy family. If you get your marriage right, you will get your children right too.

Disciple Your Children

Proverbs 22:6 promises, "Train up a child in the way he should go, and when he is old he will not turn from it." Train, disciple, discipline, instruct, teach, and equip are all words that describe a parent's responsibility for the transfer of spiritual, moral, and practical knowledge. And it is what Jesus called "Making disciples." See Psalm 78:1-7

Earlier, we wrote a disciple is:
- *called* to live "in" Christ (salvation, abiding with Him)
- *equipped* to live "like" Christ (growth, transformation)
- *sent* to live "for" Christ (love and deeds)

And this is a good framework for discipling your children.
- First, make sure your children hear the gospel of Jesus on a regular basis. And at an appropriate time ask if they would like to receive Jesus. Don't delegate this task.
- Second, show them by your example and through instruction from you and others how Jesus lived His life. Encourage them to follow His example in their own lives.
- Third, show your children what it looks like to be a man or woman of God in a world that has grown weary of talk and yearns to see authentic examples of Christianity.

Here are three practical activities which can be included in discipling your children.
- Family Devotions. This is an effective way of getting your children into the Scriptures. Keep it simple, brief and age-appropriate.
- Financial Incentives. You probably employ financial incentives to get your children to do household chores. Why not to grow in their walk? Works for personal devotions, memorizing.
- Church Attendance. Take your children to church. Should you require them to go if they don't want to go? Would you require them to go to school if they didn't want to go? Of course!

Spend Time with Them

A chief responsibility of being a father is time. If you don't have enough time for your children, you can be 100% certain you are not following God's will for your life.

Here are some practical ways which will enable you to spend time with your children.
- Set Work/Family Boundaries. If you are setting boundaries for your kids, set some boundaries for yourself also—work

48

boundaries. Or find a different job that allows you to give them quality time.

- Give Them Time How They Want It. If they like games, give them games. If they like sports, do sports with them and attend their games when they begin team sports.
- Date Your Children. Try taking your children on a date night with Dad. Perhaps out to eat, or to some activity which fits their interest and schedule.
- Eat Dinner Together. There is research suggesting that eating dinner together is a main way family values are passed from one generation to another. Always bless the food.

Pray for Your Children

You and your wife (and possibly their grandparents) may be the only people in the world who will pray for your children on a regular basis. Here are some suggested items from *The Man in the Mirror*.
- a saving faith (thanksgiving if already Christian)
- a growing faith
- an independent faith (as they grow up)
- their strength and health in mind, body, and spirit
- a sense of destiny (purpose)
- a desire for integrity
- a call to excellence
- an understanding of the ministry God has for them
- my commitment to set aside times to spend with them
- a thirst to acquire wisdom
- protection from drugs, alcohol, and premarital sex
- the mate God has for them (alive somewhere, needing prayer)
- a passion to glorify the Lord in everything

Encourage Your Children with Words

There are two statements that every child longs to hear repeatedly: "I love you" and "I'm proud of you." Tell your children every day, "I love you" and "I'm proud of you."

If they are already grown and perhaps gone, call them or email them and tell them. Tell them over and over again.

This is not without biblical precedent. When the Father came in the form of the Holy Spirit at the baptism of Jesus (Matthew 3:13–17) and also at the transfiguration (Matthew 17:1–8), what did He say? "This is my Son, whom I love."*I love you!* "With Him I am well pleased."*I'm proud of you!*

Make Your Family Your #1 Ministry

No one else cares about your family like you do. No one else can, or should, take responsibility to disciple your family. That one's on you.

Your family is your most important small group, prayer group, fellowship group, discipleship group, and ministry. Until you get your family right, you really shouldn't be doing ministry anywhere else.

Application Questions

1. If your parents are still living, contact them and thank them for all they have done for you—even if they didn't get it all right. Some of us don't have that opportunity and wish we did. Can you think of some specific things for which you could thank them?

2. Think back over the four types of fathers: the Authoritative, the Permissive, the Disconnected, and the Encouraging. If your father was involved in your life, or if you had a father figure, which of

the four types was he? What do you personally need to do now to become an Encouraging Father?

_____

_____

_____

_____

_____

3. "Do not allow what God prohibits and do not prohibit what God allows." This is a powerful and simple rule of thumb. How are you doing with it? Allowing anything you need to prohibit? Prohibiting anything you need to allow?

_____

_____

_____

_____

_____

4. Have you ever thought about how your children treat their mother? You were challenged to cherish and respect her. Do they? Do they treat her more like hired help than who she really is? Part of the way you cherish and respect your wife depends on insisting that your children do also. What do you think?

_____

_____

_____

_____

_____

5. How are you doing with sharing the gospel with your kids? The Mellichamps attended a CRU Conference in California and brought a copy of CRU's Good News comic book for both children intending to read through it with them. Ten minutes after walking into the house, their daughter ran down the stairs and announced, "I read the little book and invited Jesus into my heart!" What can you do to get your children to consider the gospel?

_____

_____

_____

_____

6. Family devotions may be the toughest part of parenting, because of the hectic pace of life many of us lead. In the Mellichamp family, Rae was responsible early on for getting baths and leading the family devotions while Peggy finished up things in the kitchen—after we had all helped to clean up after dinner. Our kids still remark about some of the books we read, **Little Visits with God** and **Winnie the Pooh** come to mind. Need to do anything here?

_____

_____

_____

_____

7. What about attending church with your children? How are you doing with that? I (Rae) had to chuckle reading about battles over going to church. It was never an issue in our family because not going was never an option. Do your children know that going to church is what you do and why?

_____

_____

_____

_____

8. Pat and Rae independently formulated the same set of rules for balancing work and family—to keep week nights and weekends free for family, leaving work at the office. Think this might be helpful for your family?

_____

_____

_____

_____

_____

9. Rae had a colleague (a professor in economics whose wife was a professor in philosophy) who commented. "My wife and I have no children and no hobbies, we work 14-16 hours a day, seven days a week—our work is our life." They were working about 100 hours a week. When we set aside week nights and weekends for family, we are working 40 hours a week. How do we compete with such people? That is not our problem. Check out Matthew 6.33. What do you think?

_____

_____

_____

_____

_____

10. Dinner together. It requires working around schedules and commitment on the part of every family member, but the dividends are worth it. It can be a time when we learn what is going on in our children's lives, what they are facing, and what their aspirations are. And it requires interest and effort on your part to make it interesting and worthwhile for them. What can you do to make this the best part of their day?

_____

_____

_____

_____

_____

Chapter 6. Friendships: Finding and Keeping Godly Friends

"There is a friend who sticks closer than a brother." Proverbs 18:24

"What's really going to help you long-term is to find a friend or two, or join a small group and live life together with a few brothers with whom you can process what comes your way."

Male friendship was a hot topic with the group of men who interacted with Pat in choosing the topics included in *The Christian Man*. In this chapter we are going to see the integral role that friendships play in God's plan for manhood, and we'll look at the practical aspects of how to start and maintain authentic friendships.

The Problem

The fallen world is tough. The accumulation of multiple unfair and unjust criticisms, insults, accusations, rejections, slights, innuendos, disrespect, offenses, bullying, being overlooked, feeling kicked to the curb, being denied access, getting ambushed, being undervalued, and getting thrown under the bus takes a toll.

The endless onslaught of trials, temptations, sins, errors in judgment, and failure wears us down. We are dulled by the wicked thoughts of our own felonious hearts. We are riddled by shame and guilt for all the ways we have let others down. It all just gets to be too much.

When men try to express their inner aches and pains—what's really bothering them—they invariably mention one or more of seven troubling symptoms.
- I just feel like I am in this all alone.
- I don't feel like God cares about me personally.
- I don't feel like my life has a purpose. It seems random.
- I have a lot of self-destructive behaviors that keep dragging me down.

- My soul feels dry.
- My most important relationships are not working.
- I don't feel like I'm doing anything that will make a difference and make the world a better place.

When Pat hears these comments, he always asks, "Do you have a best friend, or are you part of a small group?" And invariably the answer is, "No."

The big idea for this chapter is the answer. "What's really going to help you long-term is to find a friend or two, or join a small group and live life together with a few brothers with whom you can process what comes your way." A man is never more weak and vulnerable than when he doesn't have a friend or two.

How Friendship is Central to the Gospel

Friendship is a central theme of Jesus' life and teaching. He tells us to encourage each other. "Love each other as I have loved you." John 15:12-13 "By this everyone will know that you are My disciples, if you love one another." John 13:35

The only hope for a man who has been overwhelmed by life is that Jesus Christ, the friend of sinners, will be his friend and raise him from the dead and arrange for friends to set him free. Friends are not God's back up plan B. Friends are God's plan A.

We've already established that the world is going to beat you down. The only question is whether you will face that alone.

Do You Have a Friend or Two Like This?

What can you get from a friend that you can get in no other way? Check out how the Bible describes the benefits of friendship in the following verses:
- Ecclesiastes 4:9-12. Godly friends make you stronger.
- Proverbs 17:17. Godly friends love you no matter what.
- Proverbs 18:24. Godly friends are there when you need them.

55

- Proverbs 20:6. Godly friends are faithful and trustworthy.
- Proverbs 27:6. Godly friends hold each other accountable.
- Proverbs 27:9. Godly friends offer each other honest advice.
- Proverbs 27:17. Godly friends disciple each other.
- Galatians 6:1. Godly friends restore each other.
- Galatians 6:2. Godly friends carry each other's burdens.

Do you have a friend or two like those described in Scripture? Friends who would do anything for you; with whom you can share confidential thoughts; who will call you on the carpet when you are out of line; who are there for discipleship, growth, accountability and prayer; who will listen when you are weighed down?

Friendships can be enjoyed one-on-one or in small groups. Here are guides on how to initiate both.

One-on-One Friendships

How to Start a One-on-One Weekly Meeting

There is a process of initiating and building relationships. Here are some steps to take for finding a new friend.

- Just try to get together to get to know one another—possibly over a cup of coffee. If he declines, go to your next choice.
- You will need to be intentional and the one who initiates. If you click, suggest you start meeting on a weekly basis.
- Move on from meeting just to chat to meeting with a purpose—for encouragement and prayer.

Friendship in the Commonsense World

How many friendships you have is completely up to you. Just be intentional.

- Start with your wife if you are not already friends, then develop friendships with your adult children.
- Most friendships are situational—organized around a shared interest.
- And men tend to organize getting together around tasks—at work with coworkers, at the gym, or involving a hobby.

Dr. Ben Carson says, "I really believe a man would be fortunate to have two or three really close friendships in his entire lifetime."

Understand that there is a real difference between an acquaintance and a friend; also between a close friend and a circle of friends. A 2:00 am friend would be more like a brother than an acquaintance. He would be there for you no matter what—or when.

A Men's Small Group

Another way to make some 2:00 am friends is through a small group. Once you are a part of a small group you automatically have the potential of several friends without having to cultivate them one-on-one.

What if you just can't find an existing group? Here is a guide for starting your own small group.

How to Start and Sustain a Weekly Men's Small Group

- First, make a list of men you would like to have in your group. Pray over the names. Ask God to bring to mind names of men He would want included.
- Next, decide what kind of group you want to lead. The possibilities are numerous: a Bible study at church, a service or mission group, an athletic activity, a book study.
- Decide when, where, and how often you want to meet. Giving some advanced thought to these issues is worthwhile. Weekly requires more commitment.

- Next, invite the men to an informational meeting to discuss the small group. Give them the time and place and aim for about an hour for the first meeting. Be sure to cover:
  - What you are trying to accomplish and why.
  - Don't ask for a long term commitment.
  - Suggest a trial period of weeks; then extend if desired.
  - Graciously let individuals decline your offer.

The First Meeting

The first meeting is informational. Start on time and open with a brief prayer. Meet no longer that an hour or so. Have refreshments if appropriate and possible.

- Five to ten minutes. Share again the purpose for meeting. Elicit their input on the purpose statement.
- Next forty minutes. Ask each man to share where he is on his spiritual pilgrimage and what he wants to get from the group.
- Five minutes. Inspire them with your vision for the group. Let them join up as they are ready.
- Five minutes. Pass out materials if appropriate. Confirm date and place for next meeting. Close in prayer.

How to Lead an Effective Discussion

Here are some pointers for leading an effective discussion:

- Let every man speak every week. Make this happen.
- Draw out the quiet man without drawing attention.
- Don't talk yourself more than 25 percent of the time.
- Ask open-ended questions.
- Don't put anyone on the spot,

Other Suggestions to Be Effective

- Call, email, or text your men each week.
- Let them know you are interested in them individually!

- Make it a family time—a place of acceptance.
- Make it a safe place for them. Long term, low pressure.
- Be sure to end on time. Honor their time!
- After the group has jelled, host a couple's outing.
- Spend five hours per week on the group. Your ministry.
- Encourage them to be involved in a disciple-making church.

Selecting Small Group Resources

- Bible Studies. If possible develop your own materials.
- Book Studies. Unlimited possibilities. Check them out.
- Workbooks. Are great. Keep them honest!
- Accountability Groups. Use the Man in the Mirror wallet size card.

What Makes a Group Last?

- Value. Your group must meet "real and felt needs."
- Care. Caring creates the value. If you care, they will come.

Conclusion

"What's really going to help you long-term is to find a friend or two, or join a small group and live life together with a few brothers with whom you can process what comes your way."

Application Questions

1. Friends are God's Plan A. And small group involvement is an automatic way to cultivate Godly friends. If you are not presently in a small group, would you make it a top priority to join a group? Are there any groups you would like to be a part of right now? Who can you contact?

_____

_____

_____

2. Early in my career, I (Rae) was challenged to head up the "I've Found It!" campaign in Tuscaloosa, Alabama. As I challenged men to assume leadership roles in the campaign, we started meeting together one morning a week in the office of one of the men. Soon someone suggested we have Bible study in addition to our organizational time, so I started a study of the Book of Nehemiah who rebuilt the wall around Jerusalem in the time of the Captivity. It wasn't long before we dubbed ourselves the Wallbuilders. The twelve of us (Dennis, Rick, Don, Richard, Harold, Ron, Nelson, Mike, Jim Allen, Charlie and I) finished the campaign, engaging 35 churches and scores of laymen and raised a media budget of $35,000 to expose the people of Tuscaloosa to the gospel. In the process, we became best of friends and included our wives and children in regular outings. We prayed for each other and for our children and for the city of Tuscaloosa. This is the way small groups are supposed to work in God's economy. We continued together for many years and eventually many of us moved away, but are still close friends. I received a call recently from Jim Allen. He just wanted to thank me again for investing in him and discipling him through Wallbuilders 40+ years ago. Does this story challenge you? Are you inspired to start or join a group? What will you do as a result?

3. Consider the seven symptoms of being worn down by the world listed in the beginning of the chapter. Do you see that when you are engaged with other men in the way we were in the Wallbuilders, the problems behind the symptoms no longer are in play? The small group worked for all of us. What about you?

60

_____
_____
_____
_____
_____

4. Here is another story of friendships built on small groups. I (Rae) became really concerned over the lack of Christian witness from the faculty on the campus of the University of Alabama. I challenged two friends, Dave (an education prof) and Paul (a music prof), to begin to pray with me and to ask God to show us what we could do to establish a Christian faculty presence at Alabama. These efforts led to The Christian Faculty and Staff Fellowship at the university and eventually led me to challenge other professors at other universities to follow our lead. The faculty ministry of CRU (Campus Crusade for Christ) is, in part, a result of those efforts. Faculty Commons now networks thousands of Christian professors and staff on hundreds of university and college campuses in the US and around the world. Walter, John, Larry, Stan, Scott, Mike, Phil, and many others traveled the world together and became brothers in Christ as we challenged professors to find creative ways to influence their students, colleagues and institutions for Christ. See any ideas for friendship here? What is the passion that God has put in your heart? Start where you are.

_____
_____
_____
_____
_____

5. Here is a way of using book studies at work to build friendships and disciple others. When Stephen Covey's book, *The Seven Habits of Highly Effective People*, came out I (Rae) started incorporating the principles in my own life and I offered to teach the material to the men in my department. We spent about a year (one hour a week) going over Covey's material and became closer

friends in the process. The Department head even commended me for doing the study as he saw the effectiveness level of our staff increasing as a result. Do you think there might be a similar opportunity for you in your workplace?

_____

_____

_____

_____

_____

6. And here is a story of how Rae and his wife ministered together in an area of her interest. Peggy teaches English as a Second Language to internationals. She had a number of her students who were interested in Christianity and asked me if I would be up for teaching a Bible Study for them (husbands and wives) in our home. So we did that for many years, becoming close with quite a few of them. Most of them were not believers. One year, we invited them all with their children for Thanksgiving dinner. We had 35 people that day for Turkey and Dressing and all the other trimmings of an American Thanksgiving! What a blast. How might you and your wife join together in a small group for study or ministry?

_____

_____

_____

_____

_____

Chapter 7. Work: How Should I Think about My Work?

"A person can do no better than to eat and drink and find satisfaction in their own toil. This too, I see, is from the hand of God, for without Him, who can eat or find enjoyment?" Ecclesiastes 2:24-25

There is no greater feeling than to believe, "This is what I'm supposed to be doing, right here, right now—even if it is hard."

Do you have that feeling? Nothing is more normal than for you to find satisfaction in your work. That is the big idea for this chapter. Because nothing is more excruciating than a job we don't like.

The men who provided input on *The Christian Man* thought that "work" was a must issue to include in the book. They remarked, "I spend a lot of time at work. How can I find ways to continue growing at work? How can I build a dynamic career that makes a difference in the world, while providing for my family?"

In this chapter, we're going to explore where the feeling of satisfaction comes from, how you get it, and what you can do if you don't have it. So let's focus on the hours we do work and free men up to do every task, however menial, as agents of Christ for the glory of God.

Is work something we do to earn money so that we can do what is really important, or is there intrinsic value in the work itself?

A Theology of Work

Not many men have a "theology" of work. This is unfortunate, since most of us will spend about half of our waking hours each week at work if we include our preparation and commute times.

Every noble concept in the work world has been lifted straight out of the Bible, whether it's about excellence, integrity, vision, leadership, planning, execution, exceptional service and other such things.

What should we think about work?

You Were Created to Do Real Work That Makes a Difference

Work isn't merely something we endure to earn money to pay for the things we really want to do when we are not working. There is intrinsic value in work.

Why do Christians believe this? It's because of a passage in the Old Testament known as "the cultural mandate." In addition to bringing the kingdom into our culture, God calls us to tend that culture as stewards of God's creation. God has delegated dominion over creation as a sacred trust. Genesis 1:27-28

Work is part of our DNA. God designed us to do good work on earth and charged us with tending all that He has made. What an awesome privilege and responsibility!

Work Is a Calling for Which You Are Ordained by God

God doesn't just call us to salvation. He also calls us to work. God ordained Adam to agricultural work with responsibilities and authority.

If you are an attorney, you are an ordained attorney. And the same goes for any other job title which exists.

Every Vocation Has Its Dignity

There is dignity in every job, because every job makes a difference. Just ask anyone who has lived through a garbage strike.

When you think of it, many people are doing really important work, but people rarely think of it or appreciate it.

Every Vocation is Sacred to the Lord

The Bible makes no distinction between sacred and secular vocations. Do you know how many references there are in the Bible for the word "secular?" None.

There is no such thing as a secular job. Every job is sacred. The Bible throughout is clear about the holiness and sanctity of work— of vocation.

Work Is Hard Because of the Fall

Work came first, and it was good. But because of the Fall, we must do our work feeling the prick of thorns.

"Cursed is the ground because of you; through painful toil you will eat food from it all the days of your life..." Genesis 3:17-19

Work Is Not Just a Platform for Ministry; It Is Ministry

Everything we do is for the glory of God. "So whether you eat or drink or whatever you do, do it all for the glory of God." 1 Corinthians 10:31

Because there is intrinsic value in the work itself, it is not just a platform for ministry. The work itself *is* ministry. That's what produces the feeling, "This is what I'm supposed to be doing, right here, right now—even if it's hard."

Every Interaction is an Opportunity to Bring Glory and Honor to Christ

God's plan is for us to do our work wholeheartedly as a representative of Jesus Christ. Colossians 3:22-24

It's okay, even desirable to plunge yourself headlong into doing a great job.

There is Always a Higher Purpose to the Work You Are Doing

God is always orchestrating all human events, even the job we can't make sense of right now. He does so to bring us into a right relationship with Him and with each other.

God is using our work, and how we do our work, to both tend the culture (the cultural mandate) and build the Kingdom (the Great Commission).

Doing Your Work Well Is a Testimony In and Of Itself

Work done well gives us a great opportunity to reflect favorably on the Christian faith.

"Make it your ambition to lead a quiet life: ... so that your daily life may win the respect of outsiders..." 1 Thessalonians 4:11-12

It Is Good to Enjoy Your Work and Find It Satisfying

All men want to be happy. A man will feel most happy, most alive, and most useful when he is doing the kind of work he was created to do.

"This is what I have observed to be good: that it is appropriate for a person to eat, to drink and to find satisfaction in their toilsome labor..." Ecclesiastes 5:18-19

We Need to Take Work Seriously

A number of factors have changed the way people think about work today that are relatively recent in our culture.

- There are fewer positions with stable pay and benefits.
- People switch career paths multiple times in their lives.
- People are renting versus buying, so there's no mortgage.

The struggle with contentment and the whole push to find oneself make settling into a job more difficult.

Work Is a Place to Make Plans and Build for the Future, but In Prayerful Submission to God's Will

Every man has an intense desire to be significant—to find meaning and purpose in life, to make a difference, to accomplish something with his life. So it is appropriate to have ambitions.

We can pursue significance in both appropriate and inappropriate ways. The difference is not so much in what we do but why we do it—our motives.

James 4:13-15 provides sound advice for making plans in submission to God's will. And submission to God will protect us from overambition.

How to Find a Satisfying Job

What if you or someone you care about can't enthusiastically say, "This is what I'm supposed to be doing, right here, right now—even if it is hard." If you can't, then consider getting a new job.

When you start looking for a "satisfying job," Here are some important factors to consider.

Balance

Look for a job that allows you to lead a more balanced life. A job that allows time for those non-job priorities that you have identified as important.

67

A Sense of Mission and Calling

Every vocation is holy to the Lord. Find a job that gives you a sense of mission—a sense that you are part of something that will leave the world a better place.

How You Are Wired

Here are some personality descriptors which will help you find a job which motivates and challenges you.

1. Visionary	Planner	Executor
2. Innovator	Adapter	Adopter
3. Designer	Developer	Maintainer

Just select one word in each set and these traits will give you more information about the type of work you would enjoy.

Practical Considerations

Here are some practical questions which will help.
1. What are your social needs?
2. What are your health/stress needs?
3. What is your long-term vocational goal?

Wild Card

Assuming time and money were no object, what would you do if you could do anything you wanted? What would your wife think?

Occupational Ministry

Remember, every job is ministry. Unless you couldn't be happy except if working in ministry, it is probably an interesting idea, but not a calling.

Conclusion

There is no greater feeling than to believe, "This is what I'm supposed to be doing, right here, right now—even if it is hard."

Application Questions

1. Reread Question 8 on page 17 in this Guide. Can you identify with Rae's thoughts as he considered the accomplishments of his recently deceased colleague? What would you like your colleagues from work to say about you at your funeral?

_____

_____

_____

_____

2. Have you ever been in a job you really disliked? The summer after I graduated from High School, I (Rae) worked in a local plant which manufactured window screens. My job was to cut the aluminum rods which held the screen mesh in the frames. This was before OSHA and all the good safety regulations were put in place to protect workers from workplace injuries. There were no guards on the saw. All summer long it was me against the saw. I have scars on my fingers, but still have all ten. What about you? Have you had similar bad experiences which worked for good? What were they and how did they help?

_____

_____

_____

_____

3. Do you have a theology of work? Is it biblical? "You were created to do real work that makes a difference." That statement in

itself is motivating. What does your theology of work motivate you to do?

_____

_____

_____

_____

_____

4. How are you doing with the cultural mandate? Is your work helping to bring the Kingdom to the culture? Do you see yourself as tending the culture as a steward? How?

_____

_____

_____

_____

_____

5. Do you accept that you an ordained __(Fill in the blank)__? Do you feel called by God into your work? How does this calling impact your work-life? How should it?

_____

_____

_____

_____

_____

6. Os Guinness writes in *The Call: Finding and Fulfilling the Central Purpose of Your Life*, "Calling should precede a choice of job and career, and the main way to discover calling is along the lines of what we are each created and gifted to be." Have you spent time and energy thinking about your calling? What else do you need to do to understand calling? Consider reading Rae's *The Call: Discussion and Study Guide* for the book by Os Guinness.

_____

_____

_____

_____

_____

7. God wants us to have an impact for Him at work. It wouldn't make sense for us to spend half our lives in a place and have no impact for Him there. Would you agree? What are you doing to make Him known in your workplace? What would be a good starting point?

_____

_____

_____

_____

_____

8. I (Rae) had a graduate student early on in my career, before I learned how to challenge students to consider spiritual things. He went on to become an outstanding manager in the technology field. Several years after he graduated, he told me he was moving to another location. I quoted the passage from James 4:13-15 and asked him if it applied to him. It had a huge impact on him and has influenced his life for decades. We have enjoyed a very close relationship as brothers in the Lord ever since. Do you have, or can you picture having, this kind of relationship with any of your coworkers? Which ones?

_____

_____

_____

_____

_____

9. The admonition to consider Balance, Sense of Mission, and Wiring in looking for a different position is powerful. If you can check off these things in finding a new job, you are almost guaranteed to be fulfilled in your new position. As applicable, how

will you seek to ensure that these factors are taken into account in future job searches?

_____

_____

_____

_____

_____

10. Wild Card! What would you do if you could do anything you wanted and time and money were no object? Have you ever thought about this? If you have and it is exactly what you are doing, you are blessed. Even if you are not looking for a new position, it might be a good exercise to have an answer in the back of your mind, just in case. What do you think?

_____

_____

_____

_____

_____

Chapter 8. Lust: The Right Way to Deal with This Powerful Drive

"You have heard that it was said, 'You shall not commit adultery,' but I tell you that anyone who looks at a woman lustfully has already committed adultery with her in his heart." Matthew 5:27-28

The practical solution to lust for most men is to get married and enjoy regular sex with their wife.

No man is immune from the temptation to lust. As one man put it, "My three greatest temptations are money, pride, and bikinis." Any man who says he doesn't struggle with the temptation to lust is lying. Plain and simple.

The Problem

Sexual attraction is one of the most powerful, primal forces God has created. Every man feels it, undeniably. When used the way God intends, sex is beautiful, even holy.

It's not exactly news, but we live in a culture that glorifies lust and sexual immorality. It is ubiquitous. In our sex-saturated culture, it's almost impossible to watch or read an interesting story that doesn't have at least soft porn (erotic images intended to arouse).

Also not news, our sexual desire is one of the most easily corrupted and difficult to tame of all human desires. So in this chapter we are going to clarify what the Bible says about sex and lust and try to clear up some of the confusion.

We'll answer questions like, What's the difference between "lusting" and "looking"? What's wrong with looking? When does looking become lusting? What is lust? Why is lust a sin? What is the difference between the temptation to lust and lust?

If we are going to solve the problems created by the corruption of sex, we first need to understand what uncorrupted sex looks like.

God's Design for Sex

Sex is God's gift to a married man and woman so they can have children and enjoy physical intimacy with each other. The biblical passage that addresses sex most comprehensively is 1 Corinthians 7:1-9. There Paul set the boundaries for holy sex in response to questions posed in a letter from the Christians in Corinth.

Here are a few points we note from the text:
- Sexual immorality is not new. It has been around a long time.
- Marriage is God's design for sex—it's for a husband and wife.
- Married people should have sex regularly.

And the big idea for this chapter is: The practical solution for lust (and other sexual immorality) for most men is to get married and enjoy regular sex with their wife.

Paul's advice for single men is also included in the passage—abstain from sex and if that is not possible they should marry. He adds, "for it is better to marry than to burn with passion."

Having thoughts about sex is normal. It's biology. God doesn't put limits on sex; He does put limits on sexual immorality. Let's clarify.

What Isn't Lust?

As men, the main way we experience sexual attraction and arousal is through sight. But we need to be clear: seeing isn't seeking and looking isn't lusting. King David didn't go to the rooftop to look for a naked woman.

Neither is attraction sinful. Attraction is essential to procreation and the perpetuation of our species. David was attracted to Bathsheba. Normal.

When a sexual image comes on your screen (TV, computer, or mental) is that for you a temptation to lust or the sin of lust? It depends.

- It is not a sin to stumble onto a temptation. It is a fine line: thoughts are temptations, not sins.
- It's what you do next that matters. We must take personal responsibility to control attraction.

You know the story of David. He gave in to the attraction of Bathsheba, committed adultery with her. She became pregnant. David had her husband Uriah murdered to cover up the sin. The baby died. David's son attempted to take over his kingdom…

Job, the friend of God, had to deal with sexual temptation and here's how. "I have made a covenant with my eyes; why then should I look upon a young woman?" Job 31:1 NKJV

Consider making such a covenant yourself to rely on when the temptation to lust hits. Making such a covenant requires will power your will and God's power.

God's Design Does Not Include Bathsheba

Letting your thoughts linger is what puts "attraction" on track to become "lust." Lust is simply sexual desire out of control.

In David's case, even though God forgave him for his sin with Bathsheba, the results were cataclysmic. He suffered permanent and irreparable damage to his relationships.

Lust is "Mental" Adultery

Because of the Ten Commandments, everyone knows that adultery is a sin: "You shall not commit adultery." Deuteronomy 5:18. There are two types of adultery.

- Adultery type 1 occurs when a married man has sex with a woman not his wife or when an unmarried man sleeps with a married woman. (Fornication is when an unmarried man has sex with an unmarried woman.)
- Adultery type 2 was explained by Jesus in the Sermon on the Mount. "You have heard that it was said, 'You shall not commit adultery.' But I tell you that anyone who looks at a woman lustfully has already committed adultery with her in his heart."

Jesus says you don't have to commit the "physical" act to commit adultery. "Mental" adultery is also adultery. Lust is sinful because it is a departure from God's plan for sex.

Lust is seeking out ways to look at, watch, listen to, read about, or covet any woman other than your wife to arouse yourself sexually, escalated if you masturbate.

Lust is more than accidently stumbling across sexually explicit material or having a sex dream. It's you proactively seeking sexual stimulation.

If you "seek out" movies for their sex scenes so you can be aroused, that's the sin of lust. When a sex scene shows up unexpectedly, if you hit the rewind button, that's lust.

Wanting to have sex with your wife is not lust. Jesus says lust is adultery and you can't commit adultery with your wife.

Is It Wrong to Masturbate?

The Bible does not specifically address masturbation. So the material that follows is Pat's opinion and should be treated accordingly.

You can masturbate and not sin. It is normal to want to masturbate. Men are going to masturbate for pleasure. It should not be a concern with two cautions:

- Don't fantasize about women and intercourse. Don't look at pictures of women or watch videos. Why, because that is lust.
- Don't allow yourself to habitually masturbate. It is subjective to define habitual—you know if it describes your practice.

The Bible is silent on this subject, so you will need to draw your own conclusion.

What Can You Do When You Are Attracted?

When you see a beautiful woman and feel an attraction, here is what you should do. Pray for her. Pray that she would come to faith if she doesn't know Jesus. And move on.

But don't walk around the block for another look. Temptation is seeing a pretty woman. Sin is walking around the block for another look.

We need to take personal responsibility. Paul wrote, "Flee from sexual immorality. All other sins a person commits are outside the body, but whoever sins sexually, sins against their own body." 1 Corinthians 6:18

Fleeing obviously requires some self control. You will never be able to consistently flee in your own strength. It is the self-control that is a fruit of the Holy Spirit in view here, Galatians 5:22-23.

Here are some practical ideas for fleeing sexual temptation:

- If you surf YouTube for legitimate topics but habitually end up watching questionable topics, don't surf.
- If every time you check your team's score on Sports Illustrated you end up on the swim suit ads, get scores somewhere else.
- If using your phone when you are home alone leads you to search for the wrong things, don't use your phone alone.

- Don't have a regular female lunch buddy or female workout partner at the gym.
- Don't travel unaccompanied with a woman who is not your wife.
- When a sex scene starts on a TV show, change channels or fast-forward through that section.

If you are where you shouldn't be, you are more likely to do what you shouldn't do. Know what your triggers are, and don't pull them. Why intentionally flirt with disaster? Flee

If you believe fleeing is the right thing to do but still struggle, then give a brother or your small group permission to hold you accountable by regularly asking you how you are doing.

Joseph's Story: Carry Each Other's Burdens

Joseph, a fairly new Christian, confessed to his small group leader that he thought he was the only man who struggled with lust.

If you have a less extreme struggle with lust, then being a part of a small group and being open with them about your burdens will probably be helpful. Two cautions are:
- Even if you have a small group of men asking you, "Have you sought out any sexually explicit material this week?" you can still lie to them.
- Leave any group that reinforces the notion that all men "struggle" with lust so it's acceptable. Men in such groups are not likely to understand God's power to change these habits.

Steve's Story: What Can You Do If You Still Struggle with Porn?

Steve tried everything to solve his problem but nothing worked until he heard the leader of a ministry that specializes in sexual purity say, "One hundred percent disclosure in brokenness, humility, continued transparency, and confession to the people you really care about is the only way out."

So Steve did just that. He confessed everything to his wife, children, pastor, friends—everyone. It worked and he has been free of addiction to porn for several years now.

Miguel's Battle and Victory over Unwanted Sexual Behavior

Miguel is a man who struggled with sexual addiction from age seven to adulthood. Through his church and by taking some intentional steps, he has experienced victory over pornography.

Here is his take. "Tell men that they can be free from compulsive behavior, but it is going to be a lifelong battle. They are going to be tempted every day."

Miguel's Intentional Plan

- Identity. Find your identity in Christ—understand what that means and what your relationship with Him entails.
- Confession. Confess to everyone you can—all of it, get it in the light. This is tough but essential for healing.
- A Group. Focus on building a grace-based relationship with Jesus with other like-minded men
- Accountability. Tell three to five guys, "I don't want to keep secrets anymore," and ask them to hold you accountable.
- Purge. All pornographic material from your home, your devices, your social media accounts.
- Counsel. Find a good Christian counselor who can help you in this area.
- Health. Take care of yourself by following a healthy diet and getting enough exercise and sleep.
- Retreat. Go on a men's retreat with your church, especially one which has a session on sexual purity.
- Mentor. Find an older man who also struggled with pornography and is now walking in victory.

- Serve. Focus on helping others which will also cause your own healing to accelerate to the next level.
- Temptation. The best way to overcome temptation is to not put yourself in a position where you will be tempted.
- Sin. When you fail—and you will—confess to Jesus, receive His pardon, and confess to an accountability partner.

Ed Cole's "Call to Action"

Ed Cole, a pioneer in men's ministry began a men's retreat once with the following prayer:

"If you are here tonight and committing adultery, fornication, homosexuality, incest, or habitual masturbation; indulging in pornography; gratifying yourself in sexual fantasies or any other kind of sex sin, I command you in the name of Jesus Christ of Nazareth to repent, and be restored to a right relationship with God the Father by being reconciled through Jesus Christ and the power of the Holy Spirit."

A "Call to Action" Prayer

Are you struggling with sexual sins? If so pray the "Call to Action" prayer on page 193 of the book and thank Him for forgiving you and move on.

Application Questions

1. Sexual attraction is one of the most powerful, primal forces God has created. Every man feels it, undeniably. When used the way God intends, sex is beautiful, even holy. Sex is God's gift to a married man and woman so they can have children and enjoy physical intimacy with each other. There are many today who think it is okay for people to "invent" their own morality. You know the story—anything goes. What about you? Are you in agreement with God's design for sex? If so, what does that communicate to you about love, marriage, sex, and lust?

_____

_____

_____

_____

_____

2. The big idea for this chapter is that the practical solution to lust (and other sexual immorality) for most men is to get married and enjoy regular sex with their wife. If you are married, do you see the importance of this? How does it play out in your marriage? If you are single, do you see that waiting to engage in sexual activity until you are married is God's intention for you? Are you okay with this?

_____

_____

_____

_____

_____

3. It is often difficult to grasp the difference between temptation and lust isn't it? Perhaps it can be summed up best by, "When you see a beautiful woman, don't walk around the block for another look." How can you use this simple idea to keep you from allowing temptations to entice you to sin?

_____

_____

_____

_____

_____

4. Prevention is an effective strategy, so is fleeing. Early in my career (Rae) I had to be in Huntsville, Alabama, in conjunction with research work I did on the Space Shuttle Program and the Star Wars Program a couple of times a month. Occasionally, I would have to stay overnight. On one such occasion, I was finishing up my meal in the hotel restaurant when a very attractive young

woman walked in and took a seat across the restaurant. Shortly afterwards, her waiter came over to me and asked if I would like to join her for a drink. What I did in response sets the standard for fleeing! I got out of there so fast there may still be a dust cloud! Had I given in, it might have ruined my marriage and other relationships; it could have ruined my testimony; it could have cost me my university position and almost certainly would have cost me my research projects. Nothing, nothing is worth risking all that. Got a plan in place to flee when such enticements come down the pike? What is it?

_____

_____

_____

_____

_____

5. One time when our children were in Junior High School, we (Rae and Peggy) had to attend a conference in another city. We had a young married couple spend the weekend with the kids. After we returned, when the young couple had gone, our son blurted out, "Dad, wait until you see what Charlie got me!" We walked up to his room, opened the closet door, and there in all her glory was Farah Fawcett Majors in the famous poster. I nearly fell over backward! What was he thinking giving my son what may have been the sexiest poster of all time. I decided to call him the next day and give him the works for doing such a bad thing! I didn't have to call him. He called me. Said the Lord had really convicted him for buying that poster and wanted to know if our son would let him take him back to the store and exchange it for something else more appropriate. He did and we all learned a lesson about temptation. Do you have sexually tempting materials around you? Are you under conviction about them? Will you commit to exchange them for something more appropriate?

_____

_____

_____

_____

_____

6. Do you have a plan of action which includes simple strategies to employ when confronted with sexual temptations? It might be not to look at some magazines and catalogs. It might be to avoid staring at attractive women. It may be to stay away from certain places or businesses. You need some quick strategies which remove you from the temptation. Have you entered into a covenant with God similar to Job's covenant? Would you do so?

_____

_____

_____

_____

_____

Chapter 9. Culture: The Role of the Christian Man in Our Culture

"Seek the peace and prosperity of the city to which I have carried you into exile. Pray to the Lord for it, because if it prospers, you too will prosper." Jeremiah 29:7

God wants each of us to go find some unredeemed corner of culture and claim or reclaim it for the glory of Christ.

The Current Climate

We increasingly live in a peculiar, upside-down culture where opinions are given the same credence as facts. Where the opinions of the masses sway the wisdom of leaders.

You know the issues: education, school violence, protecting innocent children, the economy, federal deficits, school debt, finding a job that pays well, racism, politics, human trafficking, the environment, poverty, social justice, fatherlessness, divorce, homelessness, gang violence, immigration, social media, bullying, internet scams, sex scandals, police shootings, abortion, marriage and gender issues. These are some of the more visible issues.

If the issues facing our culture could be solved with logic, they would have been resolved by now. And the issues keep changing. Our culture today is very different from what we faced a few years ago and what we will face in the future.

Culture was definitely on the minds of the twenty-four men who gave input for this book. And they specifically wanted the book to address how a Christian man can know how he should interact with today's culture.

On what basis do I accept cultural shifts? How can I stay true to my faith when so many around me are abandoning theirs? How do I deal with social media and digital addiction? How should

Christians mix politics and faith, or should we? Why do we still have black churches, white churches, and Hispanic churches? How can I engage the culture without coming off as critical? I want to be a Christian who makes a difference, but I don't want to be belligerent about it. How can I engage with such a rapidly vacillating culture?

Here is how we will proceed. First, we'll explore how Jesus interacted with culture so we can establish the benchmark. Then we'll look at the stance of a Christian man toward culture in the current climate. Next, while we don't have space to cover every issue raised by the storyboard men, we'll look for inspiration from a couple of examples of cultural change. We'll end by helping you find or affirm your personal stance and calling to culture.

The big question for the Christian man is where in my community is my influence as a Christian needed most? And the big idea is: God wants each of us to go find some unredeemed corner of culture and claim or reclaim it for the glory of Christ.

The Stance Jesus Took Toward Culture

It is quite surprising that someone as opposed to the existing order as Jesus wouldn't try to replace it. But Jesus had no desire to overthrow or replace the existing culture.

Nor did He seek to embrace or withdraw from the culture. Instead, the stance of Jesus was to engage culture. He didn't come to install a new Christian culture. He came to "embed" the Kingdom of God into the existing culture.

Jesus focused primarily on the Kingdom of God. But He also weighed in on virtually every issue confronting His current culture including government, taxes, marriage, divorce, greed and pride.

Here is the stance He took: He met the practical needs of people, while explaining how the gospel applied to every aspect of

85

their eternal and temporal lives.

Our Stance Toward Culture

The saying "in but not of" the world comes from what we call the High Priestly prayer of Jesus found in John 17. Jesus doesn't take us out of the world. He sends us into the world, following His own example, meeting the needs of people while speaking the gospel into their lives.

The Babylonian exile beginning in 606 BC serves as a prototype of how we are to live our lives in a hostile culture. We are commanded to "seek the peace and prosperity of the city to which I have carried you into exile, pray to the Lord for it, because if it prospers, you too will prosper." Jeremiah 29:4-7

So where are we to engage the culture? Right where we are. The question to ask is, "What are the practical needs around me that are going unmet?" And what would loyalty to Christ look like in response to those needs.

An Example of Racial Reconciliation

Pat shares an experience motivated by his association with Tom Skinner, an African American Christian Leader, in which the two of them agreed to spend time together to get to know one another.

Inspired by his relationship with Tom, Pat started a multiracial group of men in Orlando. They came to care deeply for each other and began to trust one another.

They were committed to redeeming the broken corner of their city's culture for the glory of God. They helped men start full-time ministries, put others through seminary, helped others with housing needs, and even did an out-of-state retreat together.

A Call to Action: Three Week Reconciliation Challenge

If you are serious about racial reconciliation, invite one person of another color to meet with you for three weeks with no other agenda than to get to know one another.

Begin by asking each other to share how you each became a follower of Jesus Christ and what God is doing in your life today. Exchange information about each other's families, work and other interests.

Wherever you feel your community needs to be redeemed, wherever you want to reclaim some broken part of culture, go for it. It will be difficult. Otherwise that problem would have been solved by now.

The Need: More Daniels in Babylon

We have the stories of three men who influenced their foreign secular culture in Scripture: Joseph in Egypt, Mordecai in Persia, and Daniel in Babylon.

In many ways the church of Christ today is a type of Babylonian captivity. Like the Jews in Babylon, we have freedom. We have positions of power. We need more Daniels willing to go into the world and faithfully represent God in the culture.

Pat illustrates by sharing his experience with the Winter Park Chamber of Commerce and how over a period of time he and others were able to create a climate in the city such that it was "okay" to be an openly Christian executive, business owner, banker, educator, judge, lawyer, politician, doctor, accountant, realtor, salesperson, contractor or whatever.

Many quiet Christians became visible. And many men and women surrendered and re-surrendered their lives to Jesus at an annual prayer breakfast.

The Challenge

What about you? Could God be calling you to be like a Daniel in Babylon, a Joseph in Egypt, or a Mordecai in Persia?

Here's the challenge for the next generation of Christian men: God is looking for men willing to be sent and to engage with and redeem civic affairs, the education system, public service, commerce, manufacturing, service industries, the justice system, the military, government, first responders, healthcare, medicine, the trades, and every other arena for the glory of Christ.

Will you be that man? Let that be your call to action for this chapter.

Application Questions

1. An outstanding reference for this chapter on engaging the culture is *Against the Flow: The Inspiration of Daniel in an Age of Relativism* by John C. Lennox, Emeritus Professor of Mathematics at Oxford University (Monarch Books: Oxford, UK, 2015). Lennox writes, "Captured by Nebuchadnezzar ... Daniel and his friends did not simply maintain their private devotion to God; they maintained a high-profile witness in a pluralistic society antagonistic to their faith." Does this inspire you? Write your thoughts below. If you are serious about how you should interface with the culture as a Christian man, consider reading this book.

_____

_____

_____

_____

_____

2. In this chapter, as Pat addresses how he and others went about engaging the culture in their city, he didn't give a list of ten things they checked off to get the job done. He shared about how groups

with which he was involved discovered activities that naturally led to cultural engagement in a variety of attractive and effective ways. Rae advises professors who are interested in influencing the culture in their colleges and universities to meet together with like-minded professors and staff in a "think tank or research and development activity" mode to explore ways of engagement which will take advantage of the opportunities available and utilize the interests and abilities of the members of the group. Think about incorporating this approach in your areas of influence or with some of the groups with which you are presently involved. What ideas come to mind?

_____

_____

_____

_____

_____

3. A list of some of the pressing cultural issues we face is given on page 84 of this guide; it includes education, school violence, the economy, federal deficits, racism, politics, human trafficking, the environment, poverty, immigration, social media, bullying, abortion, and marriage and gender issues. Take a minute and look back over the complete list. Now consider some of the tools and techniques we have at hand to help address such issues: social media, podcasts, blogs, You Tube, websites, town hall meetings, and a host of others. Pick any topic, add a small group as a catalyst and begin to utilize some of the tools and techniques at hand and you have a powerful approach to begin to engage the culture. Does this give you some ideas about where you might begin? [The next three questions highlight some of the areas in which we are currently engaging the culture.]

_____

_____

_____

_____

_____

4. Did you happen to see the movie *God Is Not Dead*? The movie illustrates a real problem in our culture today and also suggests a fertile opportunity for Christian men to engage the culture. The story follows a young college freshman who is called out in his Biology 101 class for not embracing the standard explanation of the origin of the universe including life itself. Many young people today, as they begin college and university studies, are being confronted with this philosophy which is hostile toward other plausible explanations. We need to equip our young people to defend their faith-based beliefs before they encounter these situations as they leave home. *Legacy of Truth* is a national ministry which has as its goal to equip high school and college students to defend ideas that are being attacked today in educational circles. If you would be interested in helping your children in this area of engaging the culture, you might want to check out Legacy's web site at legacyoftruth.org and also *When Students Ask—Questions About the Origin of the Universe*, an eBook available from amazon.com. Rae is a member of Legacy's board and friend of founder Peter Bocchino. Would this be a way of engaging the culture where you could contribute? If you have children who are in high school getting ready for college it would certainly be a great way helping them ease the transition. What do you think?

---

5. This is such a huge problem in the culture today and people are so misinformed about the truth that Rae was inspired to write a small book primarily for "the man in the street" and "the kid in the classroom" which presents the truth in non-scientific terms and which can be easily read in an hour or so. *The Bible vs. Science? Or Not!* shows how the biblical description of the Creation found in Genesis 1:1-2:3 is thoroughly consistent with what we know

about the Creation from science and suggests that some of the details of the biblical account we are just now discovering from science. Is this an area that might be of interest to you and some of your friends and acquaintances? You might want to check out the book at amazon.com. This kind of information needs to be widely available to our young people, especially those who are getting ready to embark on college or university studies. It also needs to be communicated to adult Christians, perhaps through Sunday School or other educational venues in our churches. Could you see yourself and your associates engaging the culture in your city in this particular area? What might be some first steps?

_____

_____

_____

_____

_____

6. In Question 4 we touched on the notion of defending faith-based ideas. This addresses a special area of activity within Christianity called Christian Apologetics, which is equipping believers to defend their beliefs. Unfortunately, we have not done a very good job in this area, and this is one of the big reasons we are not doing as well as we need to do in the culture war. Many believers are simply not prepared to offer reasons for their faith and therefore back down when challenged. Rae is involved as a board member in an apologetic equipping ministry in the Atlanta area called *The Aeropagus* after the forum in Athens, Greece, where the Apostle Paul spoke about *The Unknown God* in Acts 17:16+. Check out the website of *The Areopagus* at areopagus.org. The Ministry hosts a website which features articles and resources, it has a blog commenting on apologetics related topics, and it sponsors a forum, featuring well known Christian speakers, which meets every other month at two large metropolitan Atlanta churches. In addition the ministry has produced an instructional course, "What Every Christian Should Know about Apologetics," or "Apologetics 101," which will enable churches to equip their members in this vitally

important area. The topics covered in Apologetics 101 include Truth, Morality, Bibliology, Worldviews, Jesus, Evil, Science, Culture, and Tactics. Is this an area which might appeal to you and your associates? It is certainly needed if we hope to engage the culture in any profound way.

---

7. Here is a funny story that communicates where we should start in engaging the culture. I (Rae) had some Law School students ask me to lead a Bible Study for Law students that would meet in the Law School weekly. So every week, I would walk out to my car drive over to the Law School and lead a Bible study. One day as I was starting out, it was like the Lord tapped me on the shoulder and said, "Rae, aren't there some students in the Business School who could benefit from a Bible study?" On the spot I decided to phase out the Law School study and start one in the Business School. We called it the MBA Bible Study and met for quite a few years. The Lord used it in the lives of many students. I heard from one of the students once that they cited a principle I had covered the night before in the Bible study in a Marketing class. Engaging the academic culture! Can it be any plainer than this? Start where God has put you. Does this give you any ideas?

---

8. Without question, the most rewarding result of engaging the culture for Rae came from one specific outcome of his involvement with the Christian Faculty and Staff Fellowship at the University of Alabama (CFF). Here is how that came about. Early

on as the group began exploring ways by which we could engage the campus culture, we became aware of a Pro-Life counseling ministry on campus and, after some investigation, decided that we would underwrite their advertising costs in the student newspaper, which probably amounted to a hundred dollars a month. After a couple of years of doing this, we were notified that a young woman who had been helped by the counseling ministry wanted to meet with the CFF. On the appointed day, this young woman showed up at our meeting with her infant son whom she had elected to keep after being counseled. She wanted to thank us for the significant role we played in helping her through a difficult time and in saving the life of her son. WOW! There wasn't a dry eye in the room that day! The best meeting we ever had before or since. This is pretty special. There are many ways in which you and your associates can influence the culture where you are. Hopefully these application questions have started you thinking of possibilities for influencing the culture where you live. What do you think? Any ideas?

_____

_____

_____

_____

_____

Chapter 10. Sharing My Faith: Authentically Helping Others Change Their Lives

"We are therefore Christ's ambassadors, as though God were making His appeal through us." 2 Corinthians 5:20

We're not trying to trick people into becoming Christians. Evangelism is simply taking someone as far as they want to go toward Jesus at that particular moment.

The Big Picture

Every Christian knows he should share his faith. Not many do. As one man said, "Sharing my faith scares and intimidates me."

This is why so many men want to know, "How can I acquire boldness in spreading the word of God."

In the chapter on friendships we saw how the world crushes everything in its path without pity and it takes its toll on men. So we need to remember that most men are far more vulnerable than they would ever want us to know.

For this reason we will emphasize that evangelism is a ministry of reconciliation. We need to treat people with love, kindness, empathy and respect.

The big idea for this chapter is that we are not trying to trick people into becoming Christians. Our goal is to take people as far as they want to go toward Jesus at this particular moment. We do this because Jesus loves them and wants them to live with Him in eternity.

In this chapter, you'll learn how we do the ministry of reconciliation. We'll discuss why we share our faith, how to start spiritual conversations, how to share your own spiritual story, and how to authentically help others change their lives in Christ.

The Great Commission

Our mission is called the Great Commission. "Therefore go and make disciples of all nations, baptizing them in the name of the Father and of the Son and of the Holy Spirit, and teaching them to obey everything I have commanded you. And surely I am with you always, to the very end of the age." Matthew 28:18-20

And here are our marching orders, "But you will receive power when the Holy Spirit comes on you; and you will be My witnesses in Jerusalem, and in all Judea and Samaria, and to the ends of the earth." Acts 1:8

Why Do We Care?

Bill Bright, founder of CRU, would often ask, "What is the greatest thing that has ever happened to you?" Then he would follow up with, "Given your answer, what is the greatest thing you could do for someone else?"

Any man who answers the first question, "To receive Jesus Christ as my Savior and Lord," will answer the second, "To help others give their lives to Jesus too."

Timeless Message, Relevant Method

Relativism is the belief that there is no absolute truth, and different people can have different views about what is moral or immoral. It is a view which is dominant in the culture today.

Another pervasive view in the culture is that of openness or tolerance. Openness requires relativism, and its aversion to any claim of absolute truth.

Given this cultural background, many Christian men are confused by the "truth" claims of Christianity. And truth claims are not going to resonate with people who don't believe in truth.

Christianity is true. We believe it is true. And not only that, we believe that using the rules of evidence it can be shown to be true beyond a reasonable doubt. But to the man who doesn't think you can know the truth, you cannot prove that Christianity (or the Bible) is true.

So how can we convince a new generation of people that Christianity is true when they do not believe in absolute truth?

A New Starting Point

We are going to need a new starting point to reach the next generation. The next generation is not asking, "What is truth?" they are asking, "What is real?" "What is authentic?" This shift from "true" to "real" is something we can use to communicate with people. Here is how:

The most powerful argument for the truth of Christianity is a changed life! Why? Because a changed life is something "real." *Your* changed life is something real. It is something that will resonate. It is something beyond dispute.

Francis Schaeffer wrote, "Each generation of the church in each setting has the responsibility of communicating the gospel in understandable terms, considering the language and thought forms of that setting." For today's generation, a more resonant starting point is not that Christianity is true but that it is real.

People Need a Guide

A man is created to love God and others, and to lead, serve, protect, and provide for his family and community. When a man doesn't understand these roles, or understands but neglects them, everyone suffers. People need what only the Lord Jesus Christ has to offer. And they also need a guide. Here is a way that will allow you to share your story with others, to guide them.

Starting Spiritual Conversations: The Golden Question

Once you have initiated a conversation with another person, after you have exchanged pleasantries and broken the ice with questions about their work and family, ask the Golden Question; "Where are you on your spiritual journey?"

This is a great question because everyone has given their spirituality some thought. And we all enjoy talking about ourselves. Ask in a sincere, non-judgmental way. Listen to their answer. Go slowly. Don't act like you have all the answers.

And then what?

Sharing Your Story: Your 3-Minute Elevator Story

Now it is your turn. Don't try to fix his problems or impress him with your theological knowledge. He doesn't care how much you know. He wants to know if you are for real.

How to Prepare a 3-Minute Elevator Story

Here is a simple outline which has guided thousands of believers to be able to quickly and conversationally share their story with another person. Each point should take about 1 minute to cover.
- Before. What was your life like before you embraced Jesus?
- How. How exactly did you come to profess faith in Christ?
- After. What has Christ done in your life since then?

Our faith does consist of propositions—direct statements about what we believe. And we believe that these propositions are true. But in most cases, reciting propositional truth isn't what connects in any generation, especially the current generation.

How, then, after telling your own story do you present the story of Jesus?

Three Essential Ideas

Here are three focusing ideas you can use to help men understand the gospel:

- God loves you very much. John 3:16
- Jesus died to forgive our sins and to give our lives meaning and purpose. Romans 5:6, Luke 9:10, John 10:10, Ephesians 2:8-9
- We become Christians when we personally confess our sins and believe in Jesus. John 1:12

Ask the Platinum Question

At this point many people are ready to become a Christian. But no one has ever asked them the Platinum Question, "Have you ever personally confessed your sins and put your faith in Jesus?"

The Final Step: The Prayer of Faith

- If they say yes, then say, "That's wonderful. How or when did that happen?"
- If they say no, then simply say, "Would you like to do so right now?"
- If they say no, then say, "I understand. Let's keep talking in the days ahead."
- If they say yes, they would like to, then say, "In that case, you can pray right now and invite Jesus into your life. Would you like to do that?"
- The answer will invariably be yes so you can lead them in a prayer of commitment.

You Are Making an Eternal Difference

Making disciples is the one idea that, once fully understood and truly believed, changes everything. Marriages, families, the workplace, our communities, our country. Everything.

Share your faith. Start today.

Application Questions

1. In Romans 10:13-15, Paul outlines how the Great Commission is to be fulfilled, "For whoever will call upon the name of the Lord will be saved. How then shall they call upon Him in whom they have not believed? And how shall they believe in Him whom they have not heard? And how shall they hear without a preacher? And how shall they preach unless they are sent..." NLB Do you understand from this and the Great Commission in Matthew 28:18-20, that God is calling on us, you and me, to reach lost people? And the way this often happens is through us sharing our faith with others as we go. Are you willing to pray for and seek out opportunities to share with people you encounter as you live your life? Who are the three people you would most like to "take as far as they want to go toward Jesus?" What steps will you take?

_____

_____

_____

_____

_____

2. One of the most important things you could do right now to equip you to share your faith is to prepare your personal testimony, or 3-minute elevator speech. I (Rae) prepared my testimony when I was first discipled through the ministry of Campus Crusade for Christ. Guess what, we used the same "Before, How, After" outline. I haven't changed the wording at all in the smallest detail in all these years. I have shared this testimony hundreds of times in every conceivable situation all over the world—one on one, in small groups, and to large audiences. If you haven't already done so, will you make writing your story a priority right now?

_____

_____

_____

_____

_____

3. Once you have completed writing your testimony or elevator speech, print a copy and put it in your wallet and save it on your electronic devices so that you can get access to it quickly. I (Rae) got on a train in Paris once and sat next to a member of a cult who really wanted to have answers to spiritual questions. I tried to engage him, but my sophomoric French was not up to the theological challenge nor was his English. Pulled out a copy of my story and left the train with him pouring over it. Easy to do once you have the story fleshed out. Will you do it?

_____

_____

_____

_____

_____

4. One thing I (Rae) decided to do early on in my teaching career was to share my faith with all of my students. Here's how. The week before the end of classes I announced that the last class would be optional and that I would cover the following points: "Who am I?", "Why am I here?", and "Where am I going?" In a typical undergrad class three quarters of the students would show up; in a graduate class, 95 percent would show. After I had been doing this for some time, some of the Christian students would invite their non-Christian friends knowing that they would hear the gospel. This kind of opportunity is rare, but I expect with some effort you could think of some way to systematically share with many of your friends and acquaintances. What do you think?

_____

_____

_____

_____

_____

5. One of the things I (Rae) appreciate about CRU is they don't just talk about sharing your faith. They do it. I've shared "The Four Spiritual Laws" on the beach in Southern California, in a bar in a

small town in Mississippi with the starting quarterback of the football team who was drinking beer and playing pinball, and through a locked screen door in the Watts area of Los Angeles and was shocked when the woman prayed the prayer of commitment at the conclusion of our conversation. God wants to use you to share your story with others. Are you available?

---

6. A number of years ago, I (Rae) led a faculty team to one of the former Soviet Republics to share research ideas with Soviet scientists. I would share some of my artificial intelligence research and conclude my talk with my personal testimony. Each of the American professors was assigned a Soviet worker to accompany him throughout the week. My man looked for all the world like a KGB agent and I can tell you that I was more than a little nervous about sharing my story. He sat on the back row and snoozed through much of my AI presentation. As I neared the end of my scientific presentation, I debated whether or not to do my personal story. I imagined him pulling a machine gun from his brief case and mowing me down. I decided, I've come half-way around the world to share my faith with these people and I am going to do it! As I launched into my testimony, my man sat bolt upright in his seat, and after hearing what I was sharing gave me a thumbs up sign with both hands waving in the air. People need to hear about Jesus. How will they hear if we don't tell them? Will you?

Afterword

The cover reads, "No man succeeds by accident. You need a plan. This is the plan." We hope you found this Discussion and Application Guide to be just that—a comprehensive plan that helped you down the road to become the man God created you to be.

We've been honored to walk alongside you and help you ponder these ideas and make changes to your life. We pray that God will give you great favor as you live your life for his glory.

Now What?

Ask a Christian man who is succeeding in life, "What's your secret?" and he's probably going to tell you, "I had a mentor." Or "A man took me under his wing and showed me the ropes." Or something similar.

There's no greater pathway to Christian success than for one man to intentionally coach (mentor, disciple) another man about how to integrate faith into all aspects of his life. That's what Moses did for Joshua, what Elijah did for Elisha, and what Paul did for Timothy. Hopefully, that's what your leader and this Guide have done for you.

You are now Paul. It's time for you to find a Timothy.

What's Next?

For a Timothy-making resource go to ChristianManBook.com and download a FREE, reproducible copy of *The Christian Man Coaching Guide*.

• You can be the coach or mentor who asks another man, "Would you like someone to help you think through the big decisions about Christian manhood?"

- You can ask a more experienced Christian man, "Would you be willing to coach me through *The Christian Man Coaching Guide?*"
- You can also work through the coaching guide with a new or existing small group.

Made in the USA
Monee, IL
16 April 2020